Creating and Using Rubrics in Today's Classrooms: A Practical Guide

Creating and Using Rubrics in Today's Classrooms:
A Practical Guide

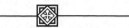

Jane Glickman-Bond and Kelly Rose

Christopher-Gordon Publishers, Inc.
Norwood, Massachusetts

Credits

Every effort has been made to contact copyright holders for permission to reproduce borrowed material where necessary. We apologize for any oversights and would be happy to rectify them in future printings.

"Key Elements of a Standards-Based System" published March 1999 by the San Diego County Office of Education, revised January 2002. Reprinted with permission.

Excerpts from the *Mathematics Framework for California Public Schools* reprinted with permission from the California Department of Education, CDE Press, 1430 N Street, Suite 3207, Sacramento, CA 95814.

All student work used with permission.

Christopher~Gordon Publishers, Inc.
Bridging Theory and Practice

1502 Providence Highway, Suite 12
Norwood, MA 02062
800-934-8322 • 781-762-5577
www.Christopher-Gordon.com

Printed in the United States of America

10 9 8 7 6 5 4 3 2 1   09 08 07 06

ISBN: 1-929024-97-5

Library of Congress Catalogue Number: 2006921719

Contents

Dedication

———◈———

We'd like to thank Principal Pat Roth for her mentoring and for never accepting less than unflinching self-reflection.

Thank you to our friends and co-workers at Arroyo Vista Charter School.

Thank you to Arthur and Louise for teaching me to learn from my mistakes.

Thank you to my mother, AnnaLee, for always believing I could do anything I put my mind to and to my father, Allan, for being the teacher I strive to be.

Thanks to Carter for his firm belief that we would finish this project, and to Aaron for his firm belief that someday we will be able to buy him a golf course.

Thanks to Zack for his advice throughout this project.

Rubrics...

Rubrics are scoring and grading tools that

Guide Instruction by:
- Clarifying individual students' strengths and weaknesses
- Making grading easier by enabling authentic evaluation

Involve by:
- Communicating the expectations of the assignment to students and parents
- Involving students in the grading process

Inform by:
- Notifying students, teachers, and parents of a child's achievement
- Educating parents and students on specifically what needs to be done to improve a score

Foreword

This book will teach educators to effectively use rubrics to guide lesson planning, instruction, assessment, and conferencing, and will effectively demonstrate the benefits of using rubric based assessments and scoring guides.

We will provide concrete examples of how to develop rubrics with all students of all age groups and abilities.

We will illustrate how the appropriate use of rubrics enhances communication between the school community and the students' homes and examine how clear communication helps to ensure every child's academic success.

This book is not intended to be a discussion of the politics of academic standards. Nor is this book intended to be an overview or introduction to the many appropriate types of assessment tools available to educators.

For the purposes of this book, we will use the term "standards" and "academic standards" to mean, "Statements of specific goals and objectives each student is expected to learn at each grade level." Different states use different terms for what we in the state of California call "standards." Some states call them "benchmarks," "grade level indicators," or "goals," as well as other terms.

We advocate critically evaluating student's demonstrated achievement of all curricular benchmarks and standards. Our experience has shown that performance-based assessments that promote critical thinking and problem solving evaluate student learning more effectively than multiple choice or fill-in-the-blank type tests. Because these assessments are only as effective as the scoring tool and the conversations that support those assessments, we have found that rubric-scoring guides are valuable tools that enhance our classroom instruction.

This book is intended to give current educators and aspiring teachers an introduction to rubric assessment tools that we, as practicing classroom teachers, have found useful to enhance parent communication and that enable us to integrate curricula, academic standards, and accountability to both parents and administration.

Introduction

The etymology of "rubric," according to the Merriam-Webster dictionary is the Middle English "rubrike," red ocher, or the heading in red letters of part of a book. It is ironic that the very assessment tool many educators are adopting is directly linked to the traditional "red pen" letter grade at the top of a student paper. The modern definition of "an explanatory or introductory commentary" is in fact closer to our current educational goal of implementing assessment rubrics.

Rubrics are a way of looking not only at assessments, but also at test taking, test giving and instruction. Rubrics guide the teacher's instruction and the students' learning and administrator's classroom observations.

Rubrics express the range of achievement possible within a class on a specific task, and set students up for academic success by clearly conveying the instructor's expectations for that particular task.

The act of creating and implementing rubrics forces instructors to clearly express the requirements of a task. We like to compare this notion to a job description. An employee should have a clear job description before he starts the job. He is then evaluated based on his performance. An employee without a clear job description will not do as well on a performance evaluation as someone who has had a job description all along.

What are Rubrics?

Rubrics are, as we use them in our classrooms, a tool for evaluating and reporting student achievement. Rubrics enable a teacher or evaluator to form an authentic evaluation of a student's achievement of a specific standard or goal. When assessing any academic objective, the instructor is looking for a certain degree of demonstrated competence (mastery) of the academic concepts.

As a result of recent "No Child Left Behind" legislation, states are required to create challenging academic standards to guide instruction. These standards lay out the academic goals, objectives, and benchmarks for each subject at every grade level. In our opinion, academic standards are not going to "go away."

Rubrics are a useful tool to use when teaching and assessing academic standards because a rubric does not show only passing or failure as other grading systems do. Well-written rubrics can show the degree to which a student has mastered the standard as well as areas of strength and need.

Rubrics can be considered a "public" evaluation system. Teachers, students, administrators, and parents should all understand what rubrics are and should have access to the rubrics. This ensures open communication between parents, teachers, and administrators as well as the students.

A well-written rubric includes "score levels." Each level specifies what the student needs to do to earn that score. There should be no guessing what it takes to pass and no guessing what the score will be if a student does less than the assignment requires. Although rubrics are used to evaluate completed tasks, a rubric also sets students up for success before the task is initiated.

All students should be familiar with the rubric before beginning the assignment, whether the task is a test, a project, or a presentation. Students then know exactly what they need to do to successfully demonstrate competency of that particular academic standard. If a student is familiar with the rubric before beginning, he or she knows what to do to receive an exemplary score, and by the same token, students know what score they will receive if they do less than the required work.

This knowledge can help lower-achieving students clarify the basic requirements and high achievers see what they can do to meet or exceed teacher expectations on academic assessments or assignments. Creating and reviewing a rubric before instruction takes place improves communication between students, parents, and teachers. There is less need to debate over why a specific score was given because the rubric clearly states how each score level was achieved. Rubrics are a more informative type of evaluation than the more subjective, traditional letter grades.

Why Use Rubrics?

Standardized tests, which are norm-referenced, compare the performance of students with that of their peers across the nation. These tests tell an assessor how well a child performs compared to other students under similar conditions answering the same questions.

Statistically, normed tests are useful in identifying children who need to receive remedial or extra services such as Special Education or Gifted and Talented because norm-referenced tests are designed to point out how extraordinary a child is, either high performing or under performing.

There is a popular misconception that statistics are infallible and that test scores are accurate reflections of knowledge. There are a few reasons we feel standardized tests are not always an accurate reflection of a child's knowledge. Any number of factors unrelated to the test can affect the outcome of this single test, including:

- School administrators, the community, and some teachers put so much emphasis on this single test that the children recognize the stress levels of the adults and become nervous themselves when being tested.

- It is one test given to evaluate all of the child's knowledge.

- The test type is multiple choice. There is no way for children to explain their answers. Students guess. If they guess correctly, it appears they understand and can apply the information, when in reality they just got lucky.

- Students whose first language is other than English may have trouble reading the test instructions as well as the content questions.

- Students may understand the concepts behind the question if it were read to them, but are unable to read the question and thus they may answer incorrectly.

- A child can be upset, sleepy, hungry, uncomfortable, or distracted.
- Students' prior knowledge and experiences differ from each other.

Although some of these issues affect any assessment given in the classroom, our main concern is that standardized testing provides only a "snapshot" of a child's performance on a given day. Rubrics, while still comparing children's abilities to one another, as do other scoring systems, provide instructional information specific to the child, which the teacher can use to guide instruction, ensuring academic success.

Rubrics can be used to gauge a child's ability to complete a specific task, based on an academic standard and then the resulting products may be compared. Each child will know exactly which components of the assessment they did well in and which areas they need more instruction in because a rubric scores each component individually. With traditional letter grades a student may receive a "B" on an assessment. The student knows they did well, but also that he or she did not completely demonstrate mastery of the assignment. A rubric specifies what a student did well or needs to improve. Rubrics are inherently a better educational tool, because critical feedback is built into the scoring system.

How Are Rubrics Used?

Our rubrics are created based on an academic goal that students are striving to achieve. We have used Grant Wiggins's "backwards mapping" model for many years. When we begin our backwards mapping, we begin our planning by clarifying the academic goal and or the academic standard being taught. After clarifying the goal or standard, identify your assessment task. The rubric is then created after the assessment has been written because the rubric should directly reflect the assessment, which directly reflects the standard. When the assessment and rubric are created, they will measure what they are supposed to measure—the student's ability to demonstrate mastery of the academic goal. Most rubrics are written specifically for each separate task, so they are valid measures of the student's achievement for each standard and will inform teachers and parents of a student's areas of strength and need. Thus, a generalized rubric that states a "student will demonstrate mastery of a certain concept" does not inform instruction nor does it clarify mastery for the student.

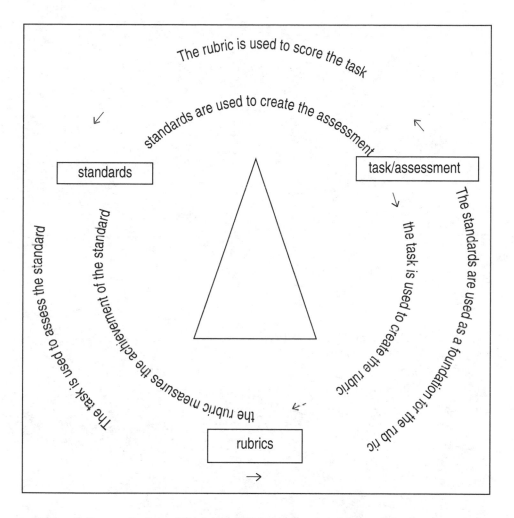

Figure 1. Demonstration of the interrelatedness the standards, rubrics, and assessments. No matter what aspect you start with on the triangle, the arrows point to another aspect that is equally important in the assessment process.

Standards, rubrics, and assessments are all inter-connected. When unit mapping and lesson planning occurs, assessments and evaluative tools such as rubrics need to be considered and developed at the same time.

Guide

Standards and No Child Left Behind

Students	Teachers	Administration
Are actively engaged in producing quality work	Are actively engaged in designing and conducting instructional activities that are aligned to standards	Are actively engaged in articulating clear goals for students based on academic standards
Are able to describe what high-quality work looks like	Make objective and valid judgments of the quality of student work	Conduct ongoing dialogues about student work
Are able to describe what assistance they need to produce high-quality work	Communicate specific expectations to students	Communicate specific expectations to staff, parents, and students
See their teachers as resources and advocates	Teach students to evaluate their own work	Teach staff and parents to be reflective of teaching practice and student work
	Understand the community's expectations for student performance and communicate the school expectations for quality work	Liaison between staff, parents, community, and upper administration/district
	Are reflective on their teaching practice and adjust their teaching practice accordingly	Design and maintain supervision and accountability
		Invest in assessments that provide credible and useful data

Figure 2. Using academic standards to promote learning. Students, teachers, and the administration share the responsibility of implementing a successful, standards-based curriculum.

All schools should have a vision of what they want their students to learn. The recent "No Child Left Behind" legislation makes it clear that academic standards "...help schools focus resources in the best way to promote learning and help parents track their child's progress."

Standards, as we use the term, are a comprehensive list of specific learning goals students will learn in each subject area, at each grade. Standards as we have used them explain what students will learn and when they will learn it. It is important that the entire school is using the same set of standards. Figure 2 shows how students, teachers, and administrators can be held accountable when using standards. Each grade level should have appropriate and differentiated standards, but there should be a spiraling sequence to the standards to ensure that each grade level is covering the necessary material to provide each child with a complete education. When a child moves from one grade to the next, the material the teacher will cover should be a continuation of what he learned in the last grade. Some states, like California, have very specific, detailed standards, which provide a spiraling sequence from one grade to another. Other states, like Colorado and Delaware, have standards that are global. We feel that standards can be beneficial educational tools, ensuring that everyone within the school has the same educational goals, so concepts don't get re-taught unnecessarily or important concepts don't get left out. These standards give teachers a basis or guide for what to teach and assess. If the school doesn't have a clear vision of their goals, the school community has no common language to compare progress and achievement.

To make a record of student progress valid, the school must be using the same standards and also assessing in the same manner. The grading system used by every teacher should be similar so the children and parents are familiar with it and know what the expectation is at each grade level. Traditional letter grades are based on percentage correct and incorrect so each teacher knows to give a "B" if the paper scores between 80 and 89%. With rubrics, because the student's ability to master different components of the task determines the score, all teachers should be clear on what constitutes each score using student work and/or anchor papers to determine mastery. A common language makes communication with the parents easier, in that parents are already aware of what constitutes "emerging," "approaching," or "mastery" when looking of assessments their child took, coming into parent-teacher conferences, or when receiving a report card/progress report.

Once a set of standards is agreed upon by the school (or state), a common language is developed, and an understanding of mastery is established, the next instructional step is to "backwards map" (Wiggins, 2000) using the academic standards or

How to Start With Standards

**Traditional instructional practice vs.
Standards-based instructional practice**

Traditional instruction	Standards/Rubric Based instruction
↓	↓
Teacher selects an instructional topic	Teacher/team select academic standard
↓	↓
Teacher selects instructional activities	Teacher/team develop an assessment and rubric that will enable students to demonstrate application of knowledge
↓	↓
Teacher designs and administers assessment	Teacher/team select learning opportunities that will give each student the opportunity to build the ability to internalize and apply new knowledge
↓	↓
Teacher gives students a grade	Teacher administers the previously decided upon assessment
↓	↓
Teacher selects new instructional topic	Teacher uses data from the assessment and rubric to either re-teach or move on to the next academic standard or concept.

Figure 3. Non-standards/rubric based instruction does not offer the opportunities for reflective teaching that standards/rubric-based instruction offers.

teacher's editions of the text you are using. This means to "start with the end in mind." As difficult as it may be to give up a favorite unit or topic of study, begin by examining the standards or the goal when planning for the year or the quarter. Plan the time (days or weeks) that is necessary to present the instruction, and the days for assessment

In a standards-based setting, the appropriate academic standard is selected, and the assessment is designed. When the assessment is designed, the rubric should be designed at the same time (or just after the assessment is created). Following this, the learning opportunities are designed or selected that will match the assessment to "set the students up for success." The other major difference is that, in our experience, a traditional classroom rarely provides structured opportunities for children to re-learn and re-assess the academic material. If a child receives a poor final score on an assessment, they are "stuck" with that score and most likely will not learn the material that they have demonstrated they need more help mastering.

When using standards and rubrics in a differentiated classroom, that is, one that is designed to meet the needs of students as individual learners, there are opportunities to go back and review, re-teach, and re-assess the material as well as extend the depth of knowledge beyond the basic concepts for those students who need to be challenged. Differentiated instruction is a philosophy of education regarding how teachers respond to the range of learners. Using differentiated instruction successfully means creating multiple paths of instruction so that students of different abilities, interests, and learning styles experience equally appropriate ways to integrate, use, and extrapolate concepts as part of the daily learning process. It allows students to take greater responsibility for and ownership of their own learning and provides opportunities for both peer teaching and cooperative learning (Theroux, 2002).

Differentiated instruction can be done by creating different activities, using different teaching techniques, or creating small cooperative groups that challenge students who have mastered the concept being assessed, or to provide support to students who are struggling with the concept. To provide this opportunity, look at an already scored rubric, which shows the areas the child mastered and those that will require more attention. The teacher can then design activities to help children try to re-learn. Then, re-assess the standards they didn't master on the assessment. It is a more thorough approach to teaching. A differentiated classroom addresses the needs of each individual student while maintaining a sense of community within the classroom (Tomlinson, 1999).

Once a teacher understands the process of planning a cohesive instructional curriculum, she can focus on understanding what each rubric requires each child to be able to demonstrate. Look at Figure 4 to see some of the key elements of planning with standards.

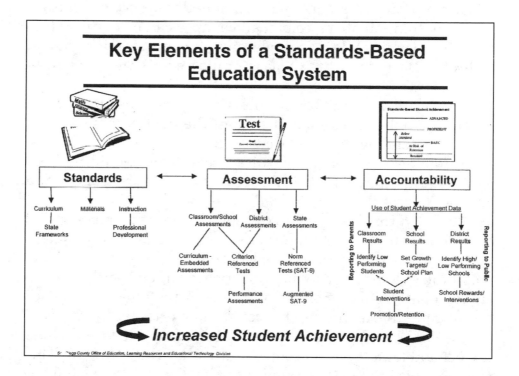

Figure 4. This graphic from the San Diego, California Office of Education shows the link between standards, assessment, and accountability. Standards are used to create assessments and assessments are used to measure achievement of the standards. Assessments create accountability for students.

Breaking Down The Standards

Though many states are now implementing academic standards, many educators are unclear on how best to assess them.

Many individual state academic standards contain more than one goal or benchmark. To properly assess each standard, the standard must be broken down. For example, one California State Standard requires that first grade students be able to demonstrate the ability to: "Describe, extend, and explain ways to get to a next element in simple repeating patterns (e.g., rhythmic, numeric, color, and shape)" (Statistics, Data Analysis, & Probability 2.1) http://www.cde.ca.gov/standards/math/grade1.html. There are three different components to this standard. For a child to successfully master this standard, he or she will have to be able to identify all three components. Being able to explain a pattern, extend a pattern and also describe a pattern using rhythm, numbers, colors, and shapes can be quite a large task for a young child. When planning for this standard, it can be broken down into three separate rubrics with three separate assessments.

One assessment addresses describing patterns that utilize rhythm, numbers, colors, and shapes, the next assessment addresses extending patterns that utilize rhythm, and numbers, colors, and shapes, and the third assessment would address explaining patterns that utilize rhythm, numbers, colors, and shapes.

Although this may seem like a lot of work, it is important to be able to report correct information. If the standard was kept intact and one rubric was created and one assessment was given, a child may know how to describe a pattern, but not be able to create a pattern. He or she may be able to extend a pattern, but not be able to explain it. This could inadvertently be reported as the child having mastered the entire standard, without having been able to master a component within the standard. This would result in the assumption that no follow-up re-teaching or tutoring would be required. In actuality, for instance, the child may not have the vocabulary to explain a pattern satisfactorily and may need to be re-taught that component.

On the same note, it is important to understand the wording of the standards. In the standard mentioned above, the operative phrase was "simple repeating patterns." For a child to master this standard means he only has to describe, extend, and explain the next likely element in a simple repeating pattern. It does not mean he has to write, draw, or create multiple elements. To demonstrate mastery, he must simply be able to name the number, shape, color, or rhythmic element that is most likely to come next when shown a pattern. When a child can accomplish more than the standard asks (in this case, perhaps naming the next element in a more complicated pattern, or extending a pattern beyond several elements) this is where the exemplary portion of the assessment and rubric come into play. This would be the section devoted to students who exceed grade-level expectation of mastery.

Both rubric and assessment design are equally important and they are inter-related. When developing rubrics and assessments, it is important that the children be able to generalize the knowledge that is stated by the standards. Students may be asked to infer a piece of information. To be able to do this, students will need practice generalizing. If the standard simply says students need to be able to read and interpret graphs, you, as the teacher will need to decide what is important to teach about reading and interpreting graphs. Students will need instruction and support with interpreting words found in the standards like "interpret," "describe," or "extend" because those will be the words most likely used during instruction as well as in the rubric.

Assessment versus Evaluation

In many ways, concerns about test scores are overtaking the process and synthesis of knowledge. We spend so much time preparing our children for testing we sometimes forget why we are even in the classroom to begin with (Cobb, 2003). Our recent classroom experiences have been that scores are being given more emphasis than process and demonstration of application of knowledge by the media and the community.

Before we move on, let's differentiate between the terms evaluation and assessment. Evaluations are done to determine what happened and resulted in a specific outcome. An evaluation is a single, final score used to report student learning. Assessment is considered an ongoing or final test used to provide information about what students learned. Assessments are used to develop instruction or interventions. Assessments can be diagnostic, like a pre-test, and formative, whereas evaluation is summative, used upon completion of instruction (Cobb, 2003).

Cobb suggests that assessments need to be useful for both students and teachers. Assessments "cannot be a guessing game. Teachers must inform students of (a) the concepts and skills necessary for achievement and more important, (b) the criteria that will be used to judge successful achievement." This statement suggests we, as teachers, should let students know what they will be assessed and evaluated on, and how they will be scored. Cobb goes on to suggest there must be feedback and re-teaching provided along with more than one opportunity to demonstrate success. Because assessment should be frequent and ongoing, short assessments are more effective than lengthy assessments.

Cobb's hypothesis is that effective instruction begins with purposeful assessments. Figure 5 is based upon Cobb's hypothesis, and is similar to our introductory graphic, Figure 1.

Curriculum	Evaluation	Instruction	Evaluation
Where do we need to go?	What do the students already know?	How am I going to get there?	What did the students learn?
Academic standards	"pre-test"	Purposefully planned learning experiences and assessments	Multiple opportunities to demonstrate application of learning
			How effective was my instruction?

Figure 5. The relationship between curricula, evaluation, and instruction should be implemented and reflected upon daily during instructional practice.

Assessment and Evaluation

Assessments should be designed after deciding what is required to demonstrate achievement. Careful development and use of assessments is crucial when using rubrics. Assessments should be designed prior to teaching, because assessment drives the content instruction. The lessons taught over the course of a unit should be relevant to the assessment so the assessment is actually measuring achievement of what was taught.

The instructor's goal should be to make sure all teaching is always geared toward the standard, but also keeping the student's prior knowledge in mind. Once the objective is laid out, the assessment is created, then the rubric is developed. By developing the rubric, the teacher can incorporate the objectives from the academic task to demonstrate mastery of the content and the academic standard.

Using an assessment as both a pre-teaching and post-teaching benchmark allows you to reflect upon your teaching practice. Looking over a pre-test can help determine what pre-existing knowledge the students have of the unit of study. On a pre-test, if most of the class has demonstrated mastery of a standard you intended to teach, you may not need to spend a large amount of class time teaching this concept. A post-test on the other hand, can show how well you were able to communicate the essential components of the standards to the individual students.

All assessments, formal or informal, are used to gather data for a final evaluation and should be ongoing. They can be pre- and post-tests. They can simply be a class discussion about a topic and noticing the information each child can share.

Special Needs

Should special needs children be graded in the same manner as regular education students? Every teacher knows each classroom contains a diverse range of learners. Each child has individual strengths and areas of need. With letter grades and multiple-choice assessments, teachers are not able to easily identify specific components of a standard that a student did well on, and which components she needs more help with. Whether students are low performing or above grade level, their areas of need will be easy to notice when using rubrics. If a student always gets the component dealing with punctuation, capitalization, spelling, and grammar scored with an under-performing mark on the rubric, it may be in indicator this child needs extra help with English language conventions—special needs student or not.

Because rubrics are based on grade level standards, it is likely students with learning disabilities (LD) and students who speak English as a second language (ESL) may not find themselves completing work at the mastery level as often as they need to.

Rubrics are standardized in that they are intended to score *all* students in the class in the same way, on the same assignment. There is no modification to the rubric for special needs students. Mainstreamed students certainly should have modifications made to assignments and special conditions applied during assessment procedures if required by an individualized education plan (IEP) or to ensure that a student is successful during classroom activities. However, if the instructor makes individual modifications to the rubric, the authenticity of the rubric is invalidated. It may be more appropriate to modify the way special needs students complete the assignment, such as tape recording an assignment, using spell check on the computer, allowing an extended deadline, or utilizing tutor assistance.

Although these students may struggle with some assignments, these students must have access to grade level curriculum in the same way as the regular education students. The 1997 IDEA law states "Many children with disabilities are excluded from the curriculum and assessments used with their non-disabled classmates, limiting their possibilities of performing to higher standards of performance" http://www.ed.gov/offices/OSERS/Policy/IDEA/overview.html. Our suggestion is to score these students on the same rubric as the rest of the class because it is a grade level assignment and all children must have equitable access to grade level material. Then the teacher can add in comments regarding the specific assignment whether the classroom teacher or another teacher who works with that child completes it.

Although all students must have access to grade level material, students with special needs are usually also receiving special education services to work on specific goals that are intended to help bring these students up to grade level. These goals are usually laid out in an Individualized Education Plan, which is drawn up by the special education teacher with input from the classroom teacher and administrators. These goals are generally not rated with rubrics, so the special education teacher along with the classroom teacher must evaluate a student's progress with regard to these goals and let parents know what progress their child is making at their appropriate developmental level. Students' IEP goals are set to ensure academic success. But they also need to have access to grade level material because that is the grade they are in and they will be able to master many of the skills you are teaching. In fact these students will sometimes master grade level work and need a challenge in a specific area.

To challenge each student and to meet the needs of each student, a teacher must know exactly which academic standards each child has mastered and to what degree. This is the only way a teacher can differentiate instruction and meet the needs of every child in today's classrooms. This works well with students who have attended the school since the beginning of the year because the classroom teacher knows what they have learned and knows their abilities. When new students enter the classroom, the instructor will be able to use pre-tests (readiness tests) to assess previous knowledge. If a student masters a well-designed pre-test, you can safely assume the student does not need to be re-taught the material and can move on to something new or more challenging.

Differentiated instruction is not limited to the regular education students or gifted students. All children excel in different areas. All learners qualify for and need differentiated instruction. If a child excels in multiplication, he will get a multiplication assignment that is more difficult than the basic assignment. This could be a student who speaks no English. On the other hand, if a gifted student struggles with geometry, he may need a differentiated assignment. This is constantly changing because all children have different strengths, weaknesses, and learning modalities.

Teachers must be as objective as possible, and must hold all students accountable to the same standard. Just because a student nearly always does exemplary work does not mean that they will ALWAYS get an exemplary score. A student who is trying his best but who is not able to meet the requirements to demonstrate mastery will not get a passing score simply because they are performing to *their* maximum potential.

We must hold all children to the same standard and provide both them and their parents with the tools to meet those expectations. For children who are in the regular education classroom, but spend part of their day in a resource or special education room, or have an IEP, we still suggest they use the same rubric as the rest of the class. Although some students may have difficulties mastering some of the grade level standards, we still want them to be exposed to grade level material and be a part of the rubric process. Parents will want to know how their children are performing on grade level material.

Before moving on to assessment and design, it's important to first point out qualifying terms that are used to score assessments. These terms are used to show the degree to which students have completed an assessment or task correctly. After understanding these qualifying terms, it will be easier to understand how to design rubrics to go with assessments. For a quick reference of all terms on a rubric, refer to Figure 6.

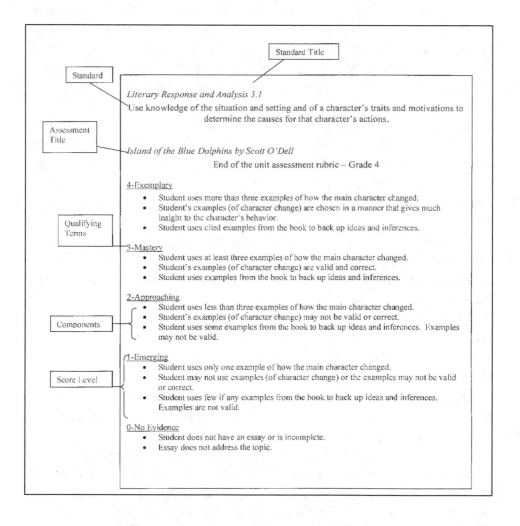

Figure 6. Sample rubric

First Steps

The first step in implementing a rubric system is getting the staff to understand how the system works. All teachers at the school site need to have a common understanding of what score levels, 0, 1, 2, 3, and 4 look like. To decide what the number scores look like, instructors should first come to an agreement on what your grading system looks like. The school community must agree on this; the goal is for two teachers to score the same paper, and yield the same score, demonstrating consistency.

What is "Mastery"?

In deciding what each number score looks like, it is essential for instructors to first agree on what the chosen level of mastery is. When writing rubrics, we found that writing the "mastery" level section first enabled us to clarify the assignment. We then write the "approaching" section, followed by the "emerging" section, then the "no evidence" section. The "exemplary" section is written last. This is the order in which we will explain these qualifying terms.

The mastery level encompasses two qualifying pieces. First, the score of mastery is awarded to students who can apply and use the appropriate academic knowledge. Mastery is the level at which teachers expect students should be scoring. Tasks designed at each grade level are tasks the teacher deems fair and reasonable for the students to complete. It is grade level work. If a student completes the task correctly and demonstrates an understanding of the task, the student will receive a score of mastery. Second, mastery is always set at 3. With a four-point rubric (4, 3, 2, 1), or a five-point rubric (4, 3, 2, 1, 0), the 3 is not the top score even though that's the score students are encouraged to achieve. The top score, a 4 is "exemplary," which is reserved for students who go beyond the grade level expectation.

Parents may think their child has not done well if he receives a 3 instead of a 4. As a teacher, you must be clear and consistent when you explain that a score of 3 is where the children should and must be when exiting that grade level. A 3 is the grade level expectation. In any of our rubrics, the components under the heading of 3 show the grade level expectation for that standard. The 4 is reserved for student work that goes above and beyond the grade level expectation, whereas numbers less than 3 are for work that is below grade level expectation.

In our classrooms, we have been using four-point rubrics. Many examples in this book will be based on four-point rubrics. As we became more comfortable with rubrics and through our own professional development, we started seeing a need for five-point rubrics. We feel that adding the 0 allowed a score for those students who did not complete or turn in an assignment, or did not display any knowledge of the standard. You may also decide to change your qualifying terms. On a four-point rubric, we commonly use "emerging" for a score of 2 and "no evidence" for a score of 1. On a five-point rubric, we use "approaching" for a score of 2, "emerging" for a score of 1, and "no evidence" for a score of 0. If you have a four-point rubric, it is quite easy to add in the fifth point. Whichever type of numerical qualifying term you use, both are valid.

There are two schools of thought regarding demonstration of mastery, which are illustrated in the Figures 7 and 8. Some people we have worked with feel that mastery must be 100% correct and any thing less is simply "approaching mastery." Another group of people feel that more than 80% correct demonstrates consistent and appropriate use of the information, and they consider less than 80% correct to be approaching mastery. Of course, there are a multitude of options for awarding percents to each number. Although we are not suggesting using percentages as the components of a rubric, we are suggesting that teachers can use percentages to help select the overall score for clarification in some assignments. A sample percentage rubric is included in Figure 7.

4 Exemplary	3 Mastery	2 Approaching	1 Emerging	0 No Evidence
More than 100%	100% correct	20%-99% correct	Less than 20% correct	Work is incomplete or non-existent

Figure 7. Sample percentage correlation between rubric a scores.

There are complications with setting mastery at 100%. First, there is little room for achieving a score of 3 since everything must be perfect to demonstrate mastery of the basic assignment. This makes achieving a 4 even more difficult. This can be looked at as a positive aspect because a score of exemplary, the score level above mastery, should be difficult to achieve because it requires exceeding the basic requirement. But if a child makes one or two mistakes on an assignment, the teacher would not be able to score it as demonstrating mastery. However, it is still possible this student has mastered this material (even with two mistakes). In the end, if mastery is set at 100%, and a student constantly makes one or two mistakes, it may look like a child is "failing to meet standards" when in fact she understands and is implementing the standard correctly with few errors.

In Figure 8, an approach more similar to a traditional grading system, but modified for use with rubrics, has been taken.

4 Exemplary	3 Mastery	2 Approaching	1 Emerging	0 No Evidence
More than 100%	90–100% correct	50–89% correct	Less than 50% correct	Work is incomplete or non-existent

Figure 8. Alternate sample percentage correlation.

If the bar is set to 90–100% accuracy required for mastery, there is room for a few errors, but it also shows students know the material well. On a rubric, this would be explained with the qualifying words. For example, one component at the mastery level might read, "Few mistakes were made," whereas at more than 100%, or a 4, it might read "No mistakes were made, and the student was able to explain his or her solution in a creative and explicit way."

We again want to state that percentages should not be the defining component of a rubric, but a clarifying component. With traditional grading systems, when a student does not turn in an assignment, he receives a 0. With our five-point rubrics, the same would apply. If the lowest score on the rubric is 1, it may imply a child turned in the assignment, but it just was not completed properly.

What is "Approaching"?

The approaching score on a rubric is reserved for students who have demonstrated some accuracy on the task, but will still need more practice and instruction before being able to master it. This is represented with a score of 2. The 2 contains a wider range of components than the 3. This is not only evident when looking at the percentage break down in Figure 8, but also in looking at the qualifying words in the components. In Figure 8, it is suggested work demonstrating 50% correctness is awarded a 2. It also suggests work demonstrating up through 89% should receive a 2. Certainly a child who has scored 50% correct understands far less than a student who has scored 89% correct. However, what a 2 tells parents, teachers, and the child, the student will need more practice and instruction in using and applying that concept whether the score of 2 represents the high end of the spectrum or the low end. The other reason there is such a wide range with the 2 is the wording of the components in the approaching section.

Looking at Figure 9 on page 32, one component of the mastery section states the, "student's math may have one or two mistakes..." The similar component for the 2 states the "student's math may have more than two mistakes..." To get the 3 the students can have specifically one or two mistakes. For a score of 2, the student could have any number of mistakes *more* than two.

What is "Emerging"?

The emerging section of the rubric is reserved for students who are performing far below grade level expectation. It is represented with a number score of 1. Students who have extenuating circumstances and who have missed a significant amount of instruction will have a hard time mastering an assessment or task. When students score at the emerging level, it is a sign they need much more intensive instruction, before they will be able to master the specific standard being assessed.

What is "No Evidence"?

The "no evidence" section of the rubric is intended for students who do not have a completed product to turn in for scor-

Area & Perimeter 1.1 and 1.4

4 – Exemplary
• Uses appropriate units with no mistakes (Standard 1.1)
• Uses formulas with no mistakes (Standard 1.4)
• Uses more than two shapes to find the area and perimeter
• Math is correct with no mistakes. Different ways to find answer
  may be used
• Written explanation demonstrates depth and understanding of
  area and perimeter

3 – Mastery
• Uses appropriate units with one or two mistakes (Standard 1.1)
• Uses formulas with one or two mistakes (Standard 1.4)
• Uses at least two shapes to find the area and perimeter
• Math may have one or two mistakes
• Written explanation demonstrates a general understanding of
  area and perimeter

2 – Approaching
• Does not use appropriate units (Standard 1.1)
• Does not use formulas properly (Standard 1.4)
• Uses less than two shapes to find the area and perimeter
• Math may have more than two mistakes
• Written explanation demonstrates little understanding of area and
  perimeter

1 – Emerging
• Does not attempt to use units (Standard 1.1)
• Does not attempt to use formulas (Standard 1.4)
• No shapes used to find area and perimeter
• Math is incorrect
• No written explanation

0 – No Evidence
• Assignment is incomplete
• Assignment is not turned in
• Assignment does not address area or perimeter

Figure 9. A sample rubric for an area and perimeter activity with specific standards.

ing or have little or no knowledge of the standard. The score awarded for "no evidence" is a 0. On a language arts or social studies assessment, this score could reflect an essay in which the student is completely off the assigned topic. This would result in a score of 0. Of course, this is a score rarely received. An effective educator does not set a child up for failure, and should be reflective during the instructional phase to ensure that as many children as possible master a concept.

If a child does not turn in an at-home project on the due date, he would receive a 0. It's then possible to raise the score once the project is turned in. (A re-assessment being allowed to raise a score). As a penalty for not making the due date without a valid excuse, we often lower the score after it has been scored with the rubric. For example, if a student received a 3 for a project, but turned it in a week late, the rubric would be filled out to show the student demonstrated mastery level work, but will also show the final score awarded was a 2 since it was dropped one score level due to tardiness. Part of our philosophy of education includes the belief that students should develop a sense of self-motivation and the ability to budget time. As a result, we weighted time management of home projects heavily, allowing our rubrics to reflect this belief.

What is "Exemplary"?

The exemplary score is awarded to students who exceed the grade level expectation. So why do we want to "break the ceiling" and encourage students to show "more?" The 4 is not just an extension of the activity with an extra 10 math problems, or an extra two pages on an essay. The 4 allows a student to demonstrate knowledge and abilities that are beyond your expectations and that demonstrate a student's ability to generalize knowledge.

Generally, a 4 should arise from a student creating something innovative or something unusual by themselves and should demonstrate depth of knowledge, not breadth. It is also important that the task required for a 4 not impinge on the next grade level's academic standards because a 4 should directly relate to the material being tested (it would not be appropriate to test quantum theory on a double-digit multiplication assessment). In the case of double-digit multiplication, a 4 might require creating a triple digit multiplication problem and then solving their own problem correctly.

When designing assessments, creating the "exemplary" section can be difficult for instructors. The rationale for an exemplary score is so that the child can demonstrate extraordinary depth of understanding of the standard. In many cases, depending on the grade level, it may be appropriate for the child to come up with a way to show his or her depth of knowledge in an Open-Ended Exemplary Section. You can simply say, "Explain to me using words and pictures something you know about division that you have not yet shown me." This allows the child to demonstrate his depth of knowledge as well as providing you with a better assessment of the child's abilities because he gets to take his own view of the question.

The exemplary section can also be achieved by providing a Teacher-Generated Exemplary Section. You can simply pose a question, task, or extension that the students must complete to earn a 4, demonstrating higher-order thinking skills, depth of understanding, and the ability to generalize knowledge. (See Figure 10 for a few examples of open-ended questions as well as teacher-generated questions.)

Open Ended
- (Make connections and demonstrate reading comprehension) Compare and contrast the main character with another character from a story we've read.
- (Extend and generalize knowledge [from single digit multiplication]) Create and solve a double-digit multiplication problem (if the basic assessment is on single-digit multiplication).

Teacher Generated
- Compare and contrast the main character of the story we just read with Karana, from *Island of the Blue Dolphins*.
- 34 x 27 = (if the basic assessment is on single digit multiplication)

Figure 10. Examples of open-ended and teacher-generated questions.

There should be agreement between teachers at each grade level whether the exemplary section will be open ended or teacher generated. In our kindergarten, students are expected to be able to count to 30. For a "4," the kindergarten teachers need to be in consensus on whether the student will be prompted by asking, "Can you find another way to count to 30?" (open ended). Or will the student simply be asked, "Can you count to 30 by 5's?" (teacher generated).

To truly offer students the ability to demonstrate creativity and innovative thinking, we believe that any questions or prompts that are offered to a student for a score of 4 should be open ended, giving a student the opportunity to demonstrate an unusual thought process or creative solution. We would ask a student "Can you find another way to count to 30?" allowing students' answers to range from counting by 5's, 2's, backwards, or in another language, demonstrating their understanding of how to manipulate numbers. We also feel it is possible that Teacher-Generated Exemplary Sections will sometimes be just as effective, depending on the standard being assessed and the type of assessment given.

When deciding on open-ended or teacher-generated questions for the exemplary section, your choice may depend on the type of assessment you're giving. Some subject areas and assessments more readily lend themselves to one type of question or the other.

Regardless of how an exemplary score can be achieved, it should be mandatory that all the children have the opportunity to try for it. We, as teachers, should always push our students to excel, and not allow them to be placed under a "glass ceiling" because of circumstances or time. There are many students to whom learning comes naturally and is never a struggle. They may not try as hard as they could because they are satisfied with fulfilling the basic assignment. These chronic "underachievers" need to be challenged as much as those students for whom demonstrating mastery is a challenge.

It's also important to note there are some skills that don't offer students an opportunity to show extraordinary depth of understanding. For example, one California kindergarten standard mandates that students be able to name the letters of the alphabet. We feel that is a discrete skill that they know or will not know. This may be an assessment that does not offer an exemplary section. Offering the opportunity to blend letters for a 4 intrudes on the next grade level's standards, this particular kindergarten grade level standard does not ask students to identify letters, or to correlate the letter to the sound (these are different standards) (http://www.cde.ca.gov/standards/reading/kindergarten.html). In no way are we denying the opportunity for a teacher to teach developmentally appropriate skills. However, your assessment should always directly match the standards that were taught. In this case, the opportunity for "above and beyond" *on this standard* may be unidentifiable, and the "exemplary" score should not be specified.

Although creating the 4 may seem to be an overwhelming part of the process, it is just as important as the other components. It provides the opportunity for students to extend, generalize, and apply their learning.

Bloom's Taxonomy and Assessments

Bloom's Taxonomy	Action verbs that can be used to create learning goals, assignments and rubrics
6 Evaluate	Appraise, choose, compare, conclude, decide, defend, evaluate, judge, justify, prioritize, select, support, value
5 Synthesis	Change, combine, compose, construct, create, design, formulate, generate, invent, originate, plan, predict, pretend, produce, revise, suppose, visualize, write
4 Analysis	Analyze, categorize, classify, compare, contrast, debate, deduct, diagnose, diagram, differentiate, dissect, distinguish, examine, infer, specify
3 Application	Apply, compute, conclude, construct, demonstrate, determine, draw, give an example, show, solve, state, use
2 Comprehension	Describe, explain, interpret, restate, retell, rewrite, summarize
1 Knowledge	Define, identify, label, list, locate, match, memorize, name, tell, underline

Figure 11. We used this graphic to be sure we were designing assessments that lent themselves to rubrics.

To help develop assessments, use Bloom's Taxonomy. In 1956, Bloom developed a sequence of levels of thinking. Bloom's Taxonomy is commonly used in curriculum development. This taxonomy can be used to develop assessment questions at various cognitive levels.

When developing an assessment, we believe that there should be a range of text questions from the comprehension through evaluation levels. Higher cognitive levels are more conducive to scoring with rubrics because knowledge questions (memorization and recall) are more objective than demonstration of synthesis and analysis of information.

The use of Bloom's Taxonomy should encourage teachers to move beyond rote memorization and recall type questions and encourage students to demonstrate internalization of knowledge by applying, analyzing, and synthesizing information.

Mechanics of Designing Assessments

So what are some rules for generating appropriate assessments when using rubrics? First, for easy record keeping, design one assessment or section of an assessment per academic goal or standard. In many cases, academic standards have three or four goals, which may need to be broken down into three or four separate assessments.

Multiple standards can be assessed at one time on one assessment. To award an appropriate score for each standard, be sure the entire standard is assessed. Each section of the assessment should be labeled with the appropriate standard for easy record keeping. Also, each standard will need to be given a separate score to ensure valid scoring. For some standards a child may demonstrate mastery whereas others may render a score of "emerging." It's important to point out some standards may need re-teaching and others will not.

The example in Figure 13 is a shortened version of a fractions pre-assessment. There are five standards being assessed so five separate scores will be awarded. There will also be one overall score awarded for the assessment as a whole.

There does not need to be a rubric with pre-assessments because you're only assessing prior knowledge, but in this case it helps to keep track of which standards children already know and which ones they will need to be instructed in. This pre-assessment covers five different standards. Some of these standards being assessed have multiple goals. To keep track of what knowledge each child already has of each standard a mastery only rubric can be created. This rubric is created of components consisting of the key descriptors of each standard set only at the mastery level (see Figures 12–14). If the child gets the problem right, he will score at the mastery level. If he gets the problem wrong, the component will not be highlighted and he will need to be taught the material before taking the final assessment.

California Number Sense Standards - 4th Grade

1.5 Explain different interpretations of fractions, for example, parts of a whole, parts of a set, and division of whole numbers by whole numbers; explain equivalents of fractions.

1.6 Write tenths and hundredths in decimal and fraction notations and know the fraction and decimal equivalents for halves and fourths (e.g., 1/2 = 0.5 or .50; 7/4 = 1 3/4 = 1.75).

1.7 Write the fraction represented by a drawing of parts of a figure; represent a given fraction by using drawings; and relate a fraction to a simple decimal on a number line.

1.8 Use concepts of negative numbers (e.g., on a number line, in counting, in temperature, in "owing").

1.9 Identify on a number line the relative position of positive fractions, positive mixed numbers, and positive decimals to two decimal places.

Figure 12. Example of five number sense standards (CA) being assessed on a final assessment.

Number Sense 1.5-1.9

3 - Mastery

- Explain parts of a whole at grade level expectation and completes problem making no mistake. (N.S. 1.5)

- Explain parts of a set at grade level expectation and completes problem making no mistake. (N.S. 1.5)

- Explain equivalent fractions at grade level expectation and completes problem making no mistake. (N.S. 1.5)

- Knows decimal and fraction equivalents making up to one mistake. (N.S. 1.6)

- Writes fraction represented by a drawing making no mistake. (N.S. 1.7)

- Understands how to use negative numbers with a number line making up to two mistakes. (N.S. 1.8)

- Can identify on a number line the relative position of positive fractions. (N.S. 1.9)

- Can identify on a number line the relative position of positive mixed numbers. (N.S. 1.9)

- Can identify on a number line the relative position of positive decimals. (N.S. 1.9)

Figure 13. A mastery only rubric used to keep track of which standards each child knows based on the pre-assessment in Figure 14.

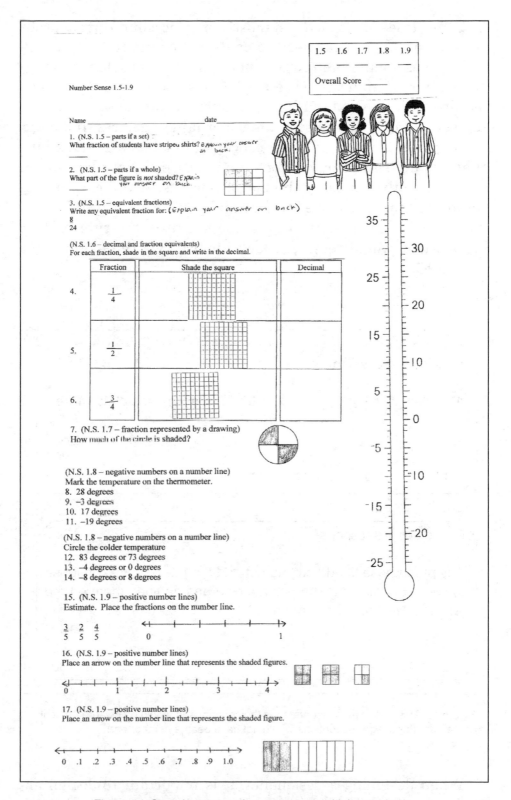

Figure 14. Sample pre-test that assesses multiple standards.

Some assessments consist mostly of basic computation problems, or problems that need to be drawn or figured out. Some math assessments can require more analysis, problem solving, and explanation. If there is a math assessment with items that require written explanations, be sure students know which subject is receiving the score: math or language arts. If a child can express mastery of math concepts, but has atrocious language and writing conventions, don't score the student down if you are only assessing the math concepts. If you can understand the math, give the student an appropriate score. Only if there is a language conventions component in the rubric, then the student would receive a lower mark. See the example in Figure 15.

Addition Assessment

A student was told to add 100 + 80. This is what the child wrote:

$$\begin{array}{r} 100 \\ +\ 80 \\ \hline 900 \end{array}$$

Explain the mistake this student made.

One student's response:

Ths prson nose to add but did not add the rite way. He iz supose to line up numbers in the bak rite side and he lined them on the left side. He shood have done this

$$\begin{array}{r} 100 \\ +\ 80 \\ \hline 180 \end{array}$$

Figure 15. This child clearly understands the concept and would be awarded a score of mastery (language conventions would not have been a component).

When designing assessments, it is important to design assessments that allow students to demonstrate quality and depth of knowledge, not simply completing a large quantity of questions. It is not necessary to demonstrate mastery of a concept by correctly completing more than five to ten problems (Cobb, 2003). If the assessment is testing long division, and a child can complete 5–10 problems correctly with few or no mistakes, statistically, the student could probably complete 50 problems correctly. When *practicing* a skill, it may be worthwhile to have a larger sample of problems. When *assessing*, there only have to be enough problems for the child to demonstrate complete understanding.

We like to focus on the use of appropriate forms of assessment. If the assessment is a multiple-choice test, there is no way for a student to achieve a score of exemplary unless there is an additional performance piece added for the child to demonstrate his knowledge because the multiple-choice test does not necessarily require a child to actually demonstrate application and generalization of knowledge.

Because assessment drives instruction, it is important to plan the assessments before the unit of study is taught. This not only helps to keep instruction on a planned path, but it also allows for you to differentiate your instruction to meet the needs of the students who come to you with more prior knowledge than expected. Once the assessment is designed, plan or design the lessons that will help reach the standard.

Look at a kindergarten example of an assessment and rubric. Our Kindergarten team began by discussing the California Measurement and Geometry standard 1.1, paying particular attention to the descriptors of shorter, longer, taller, lighter, heavier, or holds more. It was also important for us to note that the standard specifies making direct comparisons with reference objects. Wanting to set the students up for success, we first identified the key terms that the students would need to know. We initially wanted the students to be able to initiate and verbalize comparisons of short, shorter, shortest, tall, taller, and tallest. After taking a closer look at the standard, we decided that our kindergartners were not being asked to make those extensive comparisons. We planned lessons that encouraged the students to compare two objects using the descriptors of tall/taller and short/shorter.

We planned an assessment that used easily identifiable pictures and that focused on the stated comparisons of "shorter, longer, taller, lighter, heavier, or holds more." We decided that a student must be able to correctly identify all the distinguishing comparisons to demonstrate mastery of the math standard. A student who was not able to correctly identify all the distinguishing comparisons would be considered "developing" or "approaching the standard." The few students who were unable to identify at least three comparisons correctly were considered to have "emergent" math skills for this standard. Students who were able to come up with a third object to fit each comparison unprompted were considered above our grade level expectation, based on the academic standard. Those students were considered "exemplary."

Because this is a math assessment, not a reading assessment, and considering the developmental level of our kindergarten students, we agreed that all the students could have the assessment read aloud. The ability or inability to read the comparative statements would not indicate understanding or lack of understanding of the underlying mathematical concept being assessed.

The rubric in Figure 18 was created to match the assessment (Figure 16) that was based on the objectives of the standard. Notice the assessment section necessary to achieve a 4 is included in Figure 17.

Measurement and Geometry 1.1
Assessment

Compare the length, weight, and capacity of objects by making direct comparisons with reference objects (e.g., note which object is shorter, longer, taller, lighter, heavier, or holds more) http://www.cde.ca.gov/be/st/ss/mthkindergarten.asp)

1. Circle the **heavier** object

2. Circle the **longer** crayon

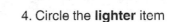

3. Circle the **taller** flower

4. Circle the **lighter** item

5. Circle the item that **holds more**

6. Circle the **shorter** animal

Figure 16. Sample kindergarten assessment.

Measurement and Geometry 1.1 (Kindergarten)
Comparing the Length, Weight, and Capacity of Objects

For a score of 4 (Exemplary Section) student must get 100% correct

To be administered verbally and individually to the student
Circle the student response.

Capacity
1. Which holds the most?   bucket,   cup,   your water bottle
    Which holds the least?   bucket,   cup,   your water bottle

Weight
2. Which is the heaviest?   Book,   egg,   cotton ball
    Which is the lightest?   Book,   egg,   cotton ball

Length

3. Which is the longest?   Your pencil,   your crayon,   jump rope
    Which is the shortest?   Your pencil,   your crayon,   jump rope

Height
4. Which is the tallest?   Giraffe,   horse,   dog
    Which is the shortest?   Giraffe,   horse,   dog

Size
5. Which is the largest?   Car,   train   bus
    Which is the smallest?   Car,   train   bus

6.
Length
Tell me something that is longer than your finger.
Tell me something that is shorter than the table.

Weight
Tell me something that is heavier than your pillow.
Tell me something that is lighter than a rock.

Capacity
Tell me something that holds more than your pencil box does.
Tell me something that holds less than our library book basket

Figure 17. This is an example from a California Kindergarten classroom. The teacher was given the option to revise the assessment and use classroom or household objects that students are familiar with to eliminate possible cultural bias.

Measurement and Geometry 1.1
Compare the length, weight, and capacity of objects

4-Exemplary
All of "3" AND for each comparison student will be able to identify additional objects that are smaller, larger; shorter, taller; lighter, heavier; shorter, longer, holds less, holds more when shown an object given by the teacher

3-Mastery
Student can correctly identify all comparisons that include distinguishing between smaller, larger; shorter, taller; lighter, heavier; shorter, longer, holds less, holds more when shown an object given by the teacher.

2-Approaching
Student can not correctly distinguish between all - smaller, larger; shorter, taller; lighter, heavier; shorter, longer; holds less, holds more when shown an object given by the teacher.

1-Emerging
Student can correctly identify less than 3 comparisons correctly.

0-No Evidence
Student demonstrates no understanding of any comparisons. Student is unable to correctly identify any comparative terms.

Figure 18. Sample rubric to go with assessment in Figures 16 and 17.

Pre-Assessment

We know to assess our students at the end of a unit, but why assess before we start teaching the unit? Before any direct instruction of a standard is begun, a pre-assessment should always be given. A pre-assessment, pre-test, or readiness test shows the instructor what knowledge the students come to the subject matter with. Therefore we usually choose to not return the pre-test to the students so they are not receiving initial negative feedback when they see how many problems they got "wrong." Students cannot identify the mistakes on a pre-test because this was new material that had not been taught yet. Instead, we used this information to guide the development of the instructional lessons based on the needs of the students depending on what prior knowledge they brought of the subject matter.

The best way to design a pre-test is to model it after the final assessment. In some cases, it may be most appropriate to use the exact same test for the pre and post assessment, or it can have the same type of problems but using different numbers like Figures 19 and 20. The following second grade example is a pre-test and post-test with the same format but different questions. The California content standard is Number Sense 5.0 [(5.1) Solve problems using combinations of coins and bills. (5.2) Know and use the decimal notation and the dollar and cent symbols for money.]

Number Sense 5.0   Name _____
Pre-test   Date _____

How much money?
1)   2)

_____   _____

3) $ .89 + $1.27 = _____   4) $34.90 − $ 1.03 = _____

5) Sara has saved $5.36 in allowance. Her mother gives her $11.00 more for her birthday. How much does she have altogether?

6) Billy has $9.22. He gave his sister $4. 20. How much does he have left?

Figure 19. Number sense pre-test.

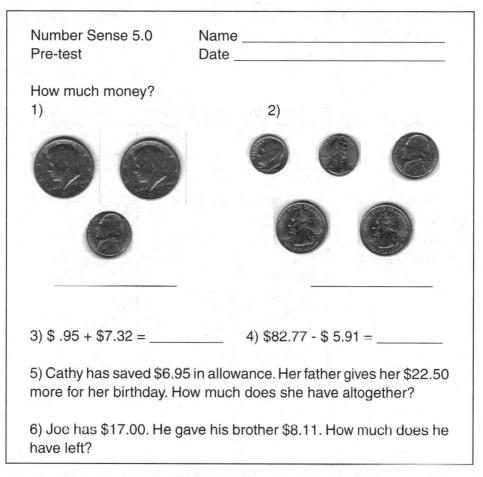

Number Sense 5.0   Name _____
Pre-test   Date _____

How much money?
1)   2)

_____   _____

3) $ .95 + $7.32 = _____   4) $82.77 - $ 5.91 = _____

5) Cathy has saved $6.95 in allowance. Her father gives her $22.50 more for her birthday. How much does she have altogether?

6) Joe has $17.00. He gave his brother $8.11. How much does he have left?

Figure 20. Number sense post-test.

A language arts, social studies, or science pre-test could be as simple as assigning an essay asking the students to explain what they know about fairy tales, Egypt, or dinosaurs. Younger students can participate in creating a KWL chart (what I Know, what I Want to know, What I Learned), filling in the "K" and the "W" initially as a class, and the "L" as the final individual assessment. Using anecdotal records, the instructor will be able to judge what a student knows about a given subject. It is important to note that while not all assessments need to be paper and pencil, it is important to have a rubric already created, ensuring more objective scores. Figure 21 is an example of a KWL chart from a third grade class in Florida. (Grades 3–5) Earth and Space: Standard 1: The student understands the interaction and organization in the Solar System and Universe and how this affects life on Earth. (http://www.positive action.net/content/PDFs/Florida_standards.pdf).

Earth and the Solar System		
K (What I know)	W (What I want to know)	L (What I learned)
• The earth is round • There are different planets • The earth spins	• How does the earth spin? • What is the sun made out of? • How many planets are there and what are their names? • Why does the moon change shape? • Why is the sun out longer on some days?	

Figure 21. KWL chart.

Figure 22 is an example from of an Earth and the Solar System KWL assessment and rubric. The student answered at least four questions correctly and his explanation was easy to understand. The instructor considered this example to have demonstrated mastery of the third grade science standard. There are some spelling errors, but spelling is not a component on this rubric, nor a part of the science academic standard. This rubric was measuring scientific knowledge, not knowledge of conventions.

10-13-03

KWL: Earth and the Solar System

What I learned:

• The earth spins on its axis. That's an imaginary line that goes through the earth. It's tilted. It spins around one time and we get one day.

• The sun is made out of gas. It is called the sun but its a star actualy. The sun makes light and heat an energy.

• Their are 9 planets. From the sun is Mercury, Venis, Earth, Mars, Jupiter, Satern, Uranus, Neptune, and Pluto

• The moon changes shape because of the way the earth, moon, and sun are positioned. When the sun shines on the moon that part looks like its lit up.

• The sun is out longer on some days because the earth revolves around the sun and if the earth is tilted a certain way as it goes around the sun the rays hit the earth at different angles.

Figure 22. An example of what one student learned after the solar system unit was taught.

Earth and the Solar System

Standard 1: The student understands the interaction and organization in the Solar System and Universe and how this affects life on Earth.

4 – Exemplary
  • Student answers all five questions and provides other information learned.
  • All students' answers are correct and show depth of knowledge.
3 – Mastery
  • Student answers at least four questions correctly.
  • Explanation is easy to understand and uses scientific language.
2 – Approaching
  • Student answers two or three questions correctly.
  • Some explanations may be difficult to understand; little scientific language was used.
1 – Emerging
  • Student answers at least one question correctly.
  • Explanations are difficult to understand; no scientific language was used.
0 – No Evidence
  • Students assessment is incomplete or not turned in.
  • Student does not address the topic at all.

Figure 23. It is clear this student received a 3 since both components are highlighted in the 3 score level.

In Figures 24–27, the pre and post-tests are the same assessment. The only difference is that the additional sections on the post-test that are not included on the pre-test (Figure 24) that will need to be completed by the students to completely assess the standards that were taught, while the pre-test is given to get a general idea of what knowledge the children already have on the subject.

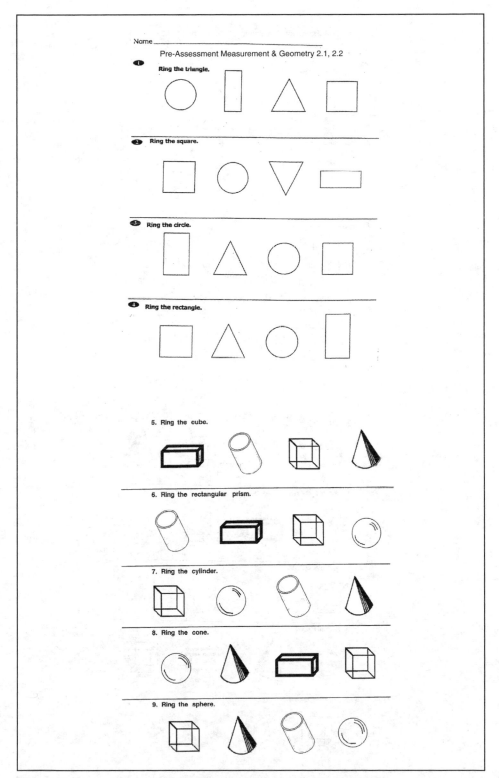

Figure 24. A kindergarten geometry pre-assessment.

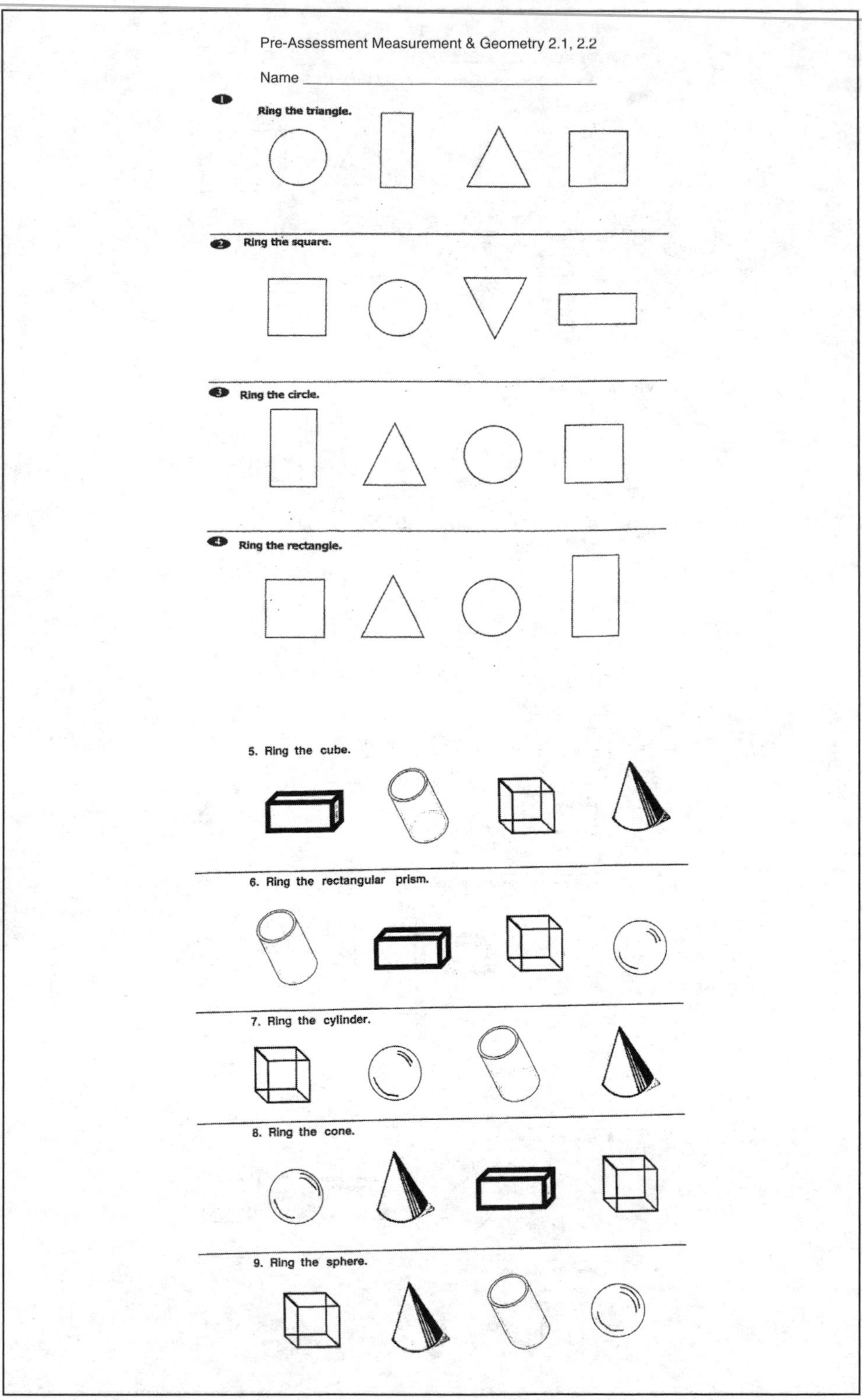

Pre-Assessment Measurement & Geometry 2.1, 2.2

Name _____

1 Ring the triangle.

2 Ring the square.

3 Ring the circle.

4 Ring the rectangle.

5. Ring the cube.

6. Ring the rectangular prism.

7. Ring the cylinder.

8. Ring the cone.

9. Ring the sphere.

Figure 25. The same pre-assessment being used as a post-assessment.

Name _____

Post Assessment for Geometry 2.1, 2.2

Show student a shape.
Ask "What is the name of this shape?
    "How do you know this is a _____?"
(Student needs to name two attributes or more.) (**1 point each**)

___ pt   1. Rectangle   _____
___ pt   2. Square   _____
___ pt   3. Triangle   _____
___ pt   4. Circle   _____
___ pt   5. Cube   _____
___ pt   6. Cone   _____
___ pt   7. R. Prism   _____
___ pt   8. Sphere   _____
___ pt   9. Cylinder   _____

Show student 2 solid shapes.
Ask " Is there anything about these two shapes that is the same? Different?"
(2 points for each question)

1. Triangle and square
___ pt   same_____
___ pt   different_____

2. Cylinder and cone
___ pt   same_____
___ pt   different_____

3. Circle and cylinder
___ pt   same_____
___ pt   different_____

Total Points (15 possible) _____

For a rubric score of 4: using provided shape manipulatives students compare the sets of shapes (1 attribute that is the same and 3 attribute that are different) **(Mark a check or a minus)**

___ 1. triangle and cone   same_____   different_____

___ 2. square and cube   same_____   different_____

Figure 26. Additional questions read to the student by the teacher in the form of an oral assessment, that are included on the post-test, but are not asked on the pre-test. It also provides part of the section to achieve an exemplary score.

Measurement and Geometry 2.1
Describes common geometric shapes

[Given one real life object for each of the nine geometric shapes, students can name 3 or more attributes]

Score 4

1. Rectangle _____   _____   _____

2. Triangle _____   _____   _____

3. Square _____   _____   _____

4. Circle _____   _____   _____

5. Cone _____   _____   _____

6. Cube _____   _____   _____

7. Sphere _____   _____   _____

8. Rectangular Prism _____   _____   _____

9. Cylinder _____   _____   _____

Figure 27. The rest of the section required for a score of 4.

By understanding what knowledge the students are starting with, lesson plans can be designed to better meet individual students' needs. If a child demonstrates that he understands and can implement the information you plan on teaching, there is no point in re-teaching the material to that particular child. The child can be introduced to Independent and Interest Projects.

Independent and Interest Projects

If the child has demonstrated mastery of the material on a pre-test, their score for this unit/standard will be a 3. Although a student may demonstrate mastery on a pre-test, they do not automatically earn a 4, nor will they want to sit through instruction of material the pre-test assessed. How does this child go about getting an exemplary score of 4? They must demonstrate extended knowledge for that specific standard. There are two options:

- Correctly complete the exemplary section on the pretest (if one is provided) or the post-test.

- Complete an Independent Project covering the same standard the pre-test covered but demonstrating a greater depth of understanding

If there is an exemplary section on the pre- or post-test, and the child passes it, he should receive a 4 as his score. The 4 section on a pre-test must be the same content and presentation as the 4 section on the post-test. By administering the same assessment, although perhaps at different times, the instructor is able to evaluate and compare scores fairly.

Independent Project

If students achieve a mastery level score on the pre-test, and there is no exemplary section on the pretest, or the child does not pass the exemplary section on the pretest, but they have still demonstrated mastery and have thus met the expectation of that standard for the grade level, he should have opportunities to be intellectually challenged. In this case the child can work on an Independent Project while the teacher is teaching the basic unit to the rest of the class.

There are many options for Independent Projects, but the activity must be worthwhile, it must be academic and it should be related to the standard being studied by the rest of the class. Prior to the start of the project, the teacher and student will discuss project options as well as guidelines for working independently. Perhaps a student who has mastered the long division pre-assessment wants to plan a party. The student researches and plans a party, and uses long division, the standard being studied, to discover the cost per person for food and favors. The student then needs to present that data, either to a peer group, the teacher or the class. If the student does an outstanding job using long division effectively and can present that information successfully (based on your pre-determined guidelines), then that student would earn a 4 for that particular standard. If you feel the student did not display exemplary qualities with the standard, she would keep a score of 3 for that unit.

Interest Project

If a student demonstrates mastery of a standard on a pre-test, but is not interested in pursuing that particular standard further, she may choose to do an Interest Project in a different subject area while the teacher is teaching to the rest of the class. This student can work on an Interest Project because she has demonstrated a mastery of depth of the standard on the pre-test. The Interest Project is a learning opportunity, but not "standardized" like activities with rubrics. This, in a sense, is a "reward" for a job well done on a pre-test. It's an opportunity for students to explore their own interests as well as an opportunity for the student to take responsibility for their own learning.

As with the Independent Project, an Interest Project and the guidelines for independent work must be agreed upon between you and the student through a conference. If a fifth grader takes a pre-test on multiplying fractions and demonstrates mastery of it, she may not want to do a "fraction project." Depending on school and parental expectations, the instructor may allow the student to take the 3 earned from the pre-test and then pursue his or her interests. Perhaps this student is interested in learning Spanish. She could work independently on a computer program learning a foreign language. The teacher and student must conference to set goals so the student is making effective use of her time and can take responsibility for her own learning by documenting time on task as well as presenting a completed project.

If a student chooses an Interest Project in a grade-appropriate curricular area, the teacher may choose to apply the project grade toward that particular subject area or standard. If a sixth grader gets a 3 on a math assessment on percent, and decides to do an Interest Project, he may choose to do some research on the architecture of Ancient Rome. Since Ancient Civilizations is a sixth-grade standard (in many states), the teacher may apply the project score toward the social studies grade. This score will not take the place of any work the student does when this standard is actually being taught, it is a score that can be added in like extra credit. The student would still participate in whole class lessons on architecture of Ancient Rome. If there was a pretest given for architecture of Ancient Rome and this particular child passed it, then he would have the same options as he did the first time he passed the pre-test.

Management of Independent and Interest Projects

Whatever alternate activity you and the student agree on, it must be something that the student can work on independently. This is because the student must be immersed in working on the project while you are teaching the rest of the class the material they did not demonstrate mastery of on the pretest. It is possible that two or more students may want to work together on the same project. This is up to you as the teacher. You'll have to be sure the students are using their time wisely and working hard on the given task. The students working on the alternative activities need to understand your rules for independent work and you will need to have a management plan if they do not follow through. (For suggestions regarding management plans, we suggest using Susan Winebrenner's excellent book *Teaching Gifted Kids in the Regular Education Classroom*.)

When the project is complete, it will need to be scored. The score is decided by the guidelines you and the student had agreed upon prior to the start of the project. If the child has met the criteria, he is awarded a 4 for an Independent Project and given credit only for an Interest Project (if the subject matter is not a grade level standard). If the Interest Project was completed in a subject area where there is a grade level standard for it, you will have to subjectively decide what kind of credit is awarded. Any score given for either project will depend on the depth of understanding the student demonstrated and the quality and creativity of the final product.

Also it's important to note an Independent Project or in Interest Project is not necessarily part of the rubric process. These projects address management and differentiation for those who have passed the pre-test and mastered the basic material. For ideas on differentiating curriculum when appropriate, see *Teaching Gifted Kids in the Regular Classroom* by Susan Winebrenner.

Independent Project

- To try to earn a "4" on the same standard tested on the pre-test.
- Decide to work on project of the same standard from the pre-test.
- Conference with the teacher for project ideas and guidelines.
- Work on project independently (or in pairs or in a small group).
- Conference at the end of the project with the teacher to discuss the score.

Interest Project

- Take a "3" for the standard tested on the pre-test ("4" cannot be awarded).
- Decide to work on project of interest—different standard from the pre-test.
- Conference with the teacher for project ideas and guidelines.
- Work on project independently (or in pairs or in a small group).
- Conference at the end of the project with the teacher to discuss the score.

Figure 28. Provides a sequence for completing independent or interest projects.

Are independent and interest projects the only options for children who have mastered the pre-test? Many teachers ask us, "Why don't you let your students go as far as they can, even if it means moving on to the next grade level's standards?" We feel this is not an appropriate option. We have two reasons why you should not encourage teaching the next grade's standards. First, we would much rather see students continue to learn their grade level standards, but explore them further; learn to generalize, find patterns, and to seek alternative applications. As a teacher, it is not necessarily our goal to accelerate accumulation of knowledge, but to increase depth of knowledge and provide varied opportunities to generalize that knowledge.

Finally, we often find that students who are gifted or constantly mastering standards quickly tend to get bored in class if not provided with a unique challenge. Many teachers may not be prepared to teach standards outside of their grade level, nor will they have the proper teaching materials. It seems in education we get caught up in trying to teach our students as much as possible. In reality we should be providing quality of instruction not quantity of instruction.

Creating a Rubric

After examining the standards and designing an appropriate assessment to test the standard, the rubric can be created. If your school or district has decided to move en masse toward rubrics, it is helpful if everyone is using the same point spread for all rubrics and that everyone has a common understanding of the descriptor that accompanies each rubric score. See Figure 29 for common qualifying terms. To facilitate parent communication as well as student understanding and use of rubrics, it is important that a school or a district share a common language across grade levels as well as across curriculum. If 90% correct demonstrates mastery in first grade, thus scoring a 3, then 90% must demonstrate mastery and score a 3 in 5th grade as well. Consistency is the key to effective use of rubrics.

The descriptors in Figure 29 are fairly general and self-explanatory. However, some terms describe the student's work (i.e., exceeding or meeting the standard) and some terms describe the student's learner qualities (i.e., consistently, usually). The term, "no evidence" is left for work that does not address the topic, has not been turned in, or is incomplete.

If students have never been scored using a rubric before, an instructor can expect the process of introducing rubrics to take up to several months. Initially, the instructor may need several months to create his or her own rubrics and score student work using the rubrics, discussing academic expectations with the whole class and conferencing with individual students regarding their work and score on tasks until finally having students become part of the process by creating rubrics and scoring their own work before turning it in to be scored by the teacher.

4	3	2	1	0
Exemplary	Mastery	Approaching	Emerging	No Evidence
Criteria Expert	Practitioner	Apprentice	Novice	No Evidence
Exceeding the Standard	Meeting the Standard	Approaching the Standard	Needs (or has yet) to meet the Standard	No Evidence
Advanced	Proficient	Basic	Below Basic	No Evidence
Goes beyond all Requirements	Satisfies all requirements	Satisfies some requirements	Satisfies a few requirements	No Evidence
Consistently	Usually	Sometimes	Rarely	No Evidence

Figure 29. Different choices for qualifying terms. The school, as a whole, could decide which set of terms will be used to keep consistency.

How Do I Know What Components to Put in the Rubric?

The rubric is intended to provide feedback regarding a student's completed work. It is specific to the task and is composed of components. The components are each individual area that is being graded. The components are laid out in each score level differentiated by degree of correctness. Each component comes from the standards being assessed and the elements of the task. The components are not created from standards alone because there are usually going to be other items you want to score based on the specific instructions of the task. The rubric in Figure 30 shows components devised from the standards and the requirements of the task.

Once the rubric is completed, the teacher can highlight (circle or underline) each component under what ever score level the student's work qualifies for. The rubric to go with any assessment should specify the academic grade level standards as individual components to be scored separately, but can also yield

Assignment

Show the area and perimeter of at least two different shapes any way you know how. Cut out the shapes from graph paper and glue the shapes down on a large sheet of paper. Show how you got the area and perimeter of the shapes using numbers and written explanations.
Measurement & Geometry Standards 1.1, 1.4

Area & Perimeter 1.1 and 1.4

4 – Exemplary
- Uses appropriate units with no mistakes (Standard 1.1)
- Uses formulas with no mistakes (Standard 1.4)
- Uses more than two shapes to find the area and perimeter
- Math is correct with no mistakes. Different ways to find answer may be used.
- Written explanation demonstrates depth and understanding of area and perimeter

3 – Mastery
- Uses appropriate units with one or two mistakes (Standard 1.1)
- Uses formulas with one or two mistakes (Standard 1.4)
- Uses at least two shapes to find the area and perimeter
- Math may have one or two mistakes
- Written explanation demonstrates a general understanding of area and perimeter

2 – Approaching
- Does not use appropriate units (Standard 1.1)
- Does not use formulas properly (Standard 1.4)
- Uses less than two shapes to find the area and perimeter
- Math may have more than two mistakes
- Written explanation demonstrates little understanding of area and perimeter

1 – Emerging
- Does not attempt to use units (Standard 1.1)
- Does not attempt to use formulas (Standard 1.4)
- No shapes used to find area and perimeter
- Math is incorrect
- No written explanation

cont.

0 – No Evidence
- Assignment is incomplete
- Assignment is not turned in
- Assignment does not address area or perimeter

Figure 30. An example of an assignment, the standard being assessed, and the rubric on one page.

one overall score. Although the rubric will give a cumulative score for the one standard, each strand of the standard is scored individually (the different components) so the child knows exactly how he did on each component. This feedback is important for students to know what their areas of strength or need are. It also allows the teacher to know what areas of weakness the entire class needs further instruction on.

Literary Response and Analysis 3.1

Use knowledge of the situation and setting and of a character's traits and motivations to determine the causes for that character's actions.

Island of the Blue Dolphins by Scott O'Dell

End of the unit assessment rubric – Grade 4

4 – Exemplary   Overall Score ___3___
- Student uses more than three examples of how the main character changed.
- Student's examples (of character change) are chosen in a manner that gives much insight to the character's behavior.
- Student uses cited examples from the book to back up ideas and inferences.

3 – Mastery
- Student uses at least three examples of how the main character changed.
- Student's examples (of character change) are valid and correct.
- Student uses examples from the book to back up ideas and inferences.

cont.

2 – Approaching
- Student uses less than three examples of how the main character changed.
- Student's examples (of character change) may not be valid or correct.
- Student uses some examples from the book to back up ideas and inferences. Examples may not be valid.

1 – Emerging
- Student uses only one example of how the main character changed.
- Student may not use examples (of character change) or the examples may not be valid or correct.
- Student uses few if any examples from the book to back up ideas and inferences. Examples are not valid.

0 – No Evidence
- Student does not have an essay or is incomplete.
- Essay does not address the topic.

Figure 31. Scored rubric based on a student's work.

Figure 31 shows an example of a rubric that has been highlighted and given an overall score. The score of 3 was given because the paper had more components highlighted in the 3 score level, than any other. The paper is more of a 3 than a 4.

Island of the Blue Dolphins by Scott O'Dell

End of the unit assessment

Literary Response & Analysis 3.1—Use knowledge of the situation and setting and of a character's traits and motivations to determine the causes for that character's actions.

Write a three- to five-paragraph essay that uses your understanding of Karana's situation and character to explain why Karana originally chose to stay on the island, but ultimately chose to leave. Be sure to include at least three examples and quotations from the text to fully explain your response.

Figure 32. Sample standard and assessment.

Literary Response and Analysis 3.1

Use knowledge of the situation and setting and of a character's traits and motivations to determine the causes for that character's actions.

Island of the Blue Dolphins by Scott O'Dell

End of the unit assessment rubric—Grade 4

4 – Exemplary
  • Student uses more than three examples of how the main character changed.
  • Student's examples (of character change) are chosen in a manner that gives much insight to the character's behavior.
  • Student uses cited examples from the book to back up ideas and inferences.

3 – Mastery
  • Student uses at least three examples of how the main character changed.
  • Student's examples (of character change) are valid and correct.
  • Student uses examples from the book to back up ideas and inferences.

2 – Approaching
  • Student uses less than three examples of how the main character changed.
  • Student's examples (of character change) may not be valid or correct.
  • Student uses some examples from the book to back up ideas and inferences. Examples may not be valid.

1 – Emerging
  • Student uses only one example of how the main character changed.
  • Student may not use examples (of character change) or the examples may not be valid or correct.
  • Student uses few if any examples from the book to back up ideas and inferences. Examples are not valid.

0 – No Evidence
  • Student does not have an essay or is incomplete.
  • Essay does not address the topic.

Figure 33. Sample standard and rubric to accompany Figure 32.

This fourth grade assessment asks students to demonstrate their understanding of the book *Island of the Blue Dolphins* by analyzing the main character and the choices she made over the course of the book. If the students understood the book, and you've practiced describing how characters change over the course of time within other books you've read, they will be able to explain what changes Karana went through and why those changes were important to the development of her character. See the rubric in Figure 33 for this assessment.

The literary analysis assessment in Figure 32 is asking students to discuss character traits and motivation. The rubric could easily include components of a well-written essay such as conventions, spelling, and writing flow and fluency. This could make the rubric more holistic and useful as a writing assessment as well as a literary analysis assessment. But this piece is specifically used as an assessment of literary analysis.

If this teacher was going to assess English language conventions and included a component for it in the rubric, conventions would have to receive a separate score since it is a different standard than literary analysis. Again, one score can be given for the assessment as a whole, but for grade-keeping purposes, it will require two separate scores. When giving the overall score be sure to keep in mind how much the literary analysis section and conventions section is weighted. If the literary analysis is inconsistent, but the conventions are perfect, it doesn't mean the overall score will be a 3. The literary analysis section has more weight because it has more components and that is the focus of the assessment. See the rubric in Figure 34 to see how English language conventions can be added into the rubric.

Another benefit of performance-based assessments and rubrics is that they show how well a child can apply and generalize knowledge opposed to how well a child can take a test. Many tests that assign grades have questions that have only one correct answer. This limits how a child can demonstrate her ability. A performance-based assessment allows a child to not only demonstrate her ability, but also to demonstrate the extension of his or her knowledge. The ability level demonstrated can be shown with a rubric since the components show a range from no evidence (will need more instruction) to exemplary (above the expected standard of performance).

Island of the Blue Dolphins by Scott O 'Dell

End of the unit assessment rubric – Grade 4

Literary Response and Analysis 3.1

overall score _____

Literary analysis score _____

Conventions score _____

Use knowledge of the situation and setting and of a character's traits and motivations to determine the causes for that character's actions.

Written and Oral English Language Conventions 1.0

Students write and speak with a command of standard English conventions appropriate to this grade level.

4 – Exemplary
- Student uses more than three examples of how the main character changed.
- Student's examples (of character change) are chosen in a manner that gives much insight to the character's behavior.
- Student uses cited examples from the book to back up ideas and inferences.
- **Student has no errors in English language conventions.**

3 – Mastery
- Student uses at least three examples of how the main character changed.
- Student's examples (of character change) are valid and correct.
- Student uses examples from the book to back up ideas and inferences.
- **Student has few errors in English language conventions.**

2 – Approaching
- Student uses less than three examples of how the main character changed.
- Student's examples (of character change) may not be valid or correct.
- Student uses some examples from the book to back up ideas and inferences. Examples may not be valid.
- **Student has some errors in English language conventions, but it does not interfere with the readers ability to read the paper.**

cont.

1 – Emerging
- Student uses only one example of how the main character changed.
- Student may not use examples (of character change) or the examples may not be valid or correct.
- Student uses few if any examples from the book to back up ideas and inferences. Examples are not valid.
- **Student has many errors in English language conventions, that interfere with the readers ability to read the paper.**

0 – No Evidence
- Student does not have an essay or is incomplete.
- Essay does not address the topic.

Figure 34. How to provide an overall score for a task and how to provide separate scores for separate standards.

We found rubrics to be an effective communication tool even when scoring math assessments. Rather than focusing on percentage of correct answers or a letter grade, we thought it a helpful tool to reflect on our teaching practice by using a rubric to break down the components of a given math concept. A well-written, generalized math rubric could look like that shown in Figure 35.

The rubric in Figure 35 is to be used with math assessments that require a written explanation. A math assessment consisting solely of twenty double-digit multiplication problems does not seem to lend itself to a rubric. Initially, it would appear to be simpler to use a percentage correct grading system. However, the rubric lends itself to educating not only the student but also the teacher about what the student is able to remember, apply, and explain.

General Math Rubric

4 – Exemplary
- Student consistently demonstrates understanding of math concepts beyond expectations with no mistakes
- Student is able to use more than one way to solve a problem
- Student demonstrates several ways to show thinking (charts, diagrams, etc.)
- Student writes clear and insightful explanations of how the problem was solved, including his or her thinking process

3 – Mastery
- Student consistently demonstrates good understanding of math concepts making few mistakes
- Student is able to use at least one way to solve a problem
- Student is able to demonstrate thinking (charts, diagrams, etc.)
- Student writes a clear explanation of how the problem was solved, including his or her thinking process

2 – Approaching
- Student shows partial understanding of math concepts and makes many mistakes
- Student is able to use only one way to solve a problem
- Student is unable to demonstrate his or her thinking
- Student writes an unclear explanation of how he or she solved the problem, or is unable to explain his or her thinking

1 - Emerging
- No evidence of understanding is displayed
- No evidence of understanding is displayed in the problem solving
- Student needs individual clarification and re-teaching of concepts

Figure 35. General math rubric.

The teacher must identify the components of a multiplication problem. One way to create this rubric would be to look at the steps used to solve double-digit multiplication problems and assign rubric scores based on the steps performed correctly. There are many different procedures for working out double-digit multiplication. The example given is for the most commonly used procedure used to teach computation of double-digit multiplication. For instance, the student must:

a) multiply the ones digit of the bottom number by the ones digit of the top number

```
        12
x       79        9 x 2 = 18
         8
```

b) carry if necessary

```
         1
        12
x       79
         8
```

c) multiply the ones digit on the bottom number by the tens digit of the top number

d) remember to add the number may have been carried,

```
         1
        12
x       79        9 x 1 = 9
       108           9 + 1 = 10
```

e) write in the 0 for a place holder,

```
         1
        12
x       79
       108
         0
```

f) repeat the process with the tens digit of the bottom number,

```
         1
        12
x       79
       108
     + 840
```

g) add the products correctly.

```
         1
        12
x       79
       108
     + 840
       948
```

When the teacher can identify all the steps necessary to complete the multiplication problem, she can transfer them to a rubric. In this case, either the student can perform the discreet skills or they cannot so there is only one score level: mastery. This rubric looks at process. To inform your instruction, it's important to look at each student's process and see where mistakes are being made. That makes it easier for the teacher to go back and provide more instruction that will fill in the gaps so students will be able to master the concept. If the teacher is solely interested in whether the answers are correct or not, this rubric would not work and a percentage score would suffice, but would not provide the critical feedback necessary to inform valid instruction.

Rubric

Double-Digit Multiplication

3 – Mastery

   Multiplies the proper digit together.

   Basic multiplication is correct.

   "Carries" if necessary.

   Writes in a place holder.

   Lines up numbers properly.

   Adds products correctly.

Figure 36. An example of a mastery only rubric.

Certainly there are alternative steps to complete a double-digit multiplication problem. If a teacher has taught double-digit multiplication in a different way, the rubric would be created the same way as the example above; list the steps and those steps become the components.

As math instructors, we always ask the question, "What if the student makes a computational error, but has the process correct?" This is something you will have to build into the rubric. In the above example, computation is addressed (basic multiplication is correct, adds products correctly) and needs to be right to achieve a score of mastery. Ultimately, all math concepts require computation to be correct, but some math concepts do not need the focus to be computation (i.e., mathematical reasoning). Within the rubric we add a component that says, "most basic multiplication is correct" for a 3. The qualifying words, " most basic" leaves room for some essentially insignificant errors.

Once you give and score the assessment with a rubric by highlighting the components the child has achieved, you will be able to identify which step many students are consistently completing correctly or consistently making mistakes with. This builds in teacher self-reflection and ensures that you are re-teaching the proper components. When using a traditional grading system, you may decide that the majority of the class needs re-teaching if the students scored under 80%. But do the students need help with the multiplication steps? Do they need help with understanding what a place-holder is? Or do they simply need to practice their basic multiplication or addition facts?

It is likely that not all students will need help with the same components. Some students may need help with carrying, and some students may need help with knowing what numbers to multiply. In this case you can break down your re-teaching into small instructional groups and pull them aside when the rest of the class is working independently. You will not need to spend any whole class time re-teaching concepts that not every class member needs. By knowing what your students need extra help with, you can focus your teaching and optimize your instructional time.

Rubric	Rubric
Double-Digit Multiplication	Double-Digit Multiplication
3 – Mastery	3 – Mastery
• Multiplies the proper digit together.	• Multiplies the proper digit together.
• Basic multiplication is correct.	• Basic multiplication is correct.
• "Carries" if necessary.	• "Carries" if necessary.
• Writes in a place holder.	• Writes in a place holder.
• Lines up numbers properly.	• Lines up numbers properly.
• Adds products correctly.	• Adds products correctly.

Rubric
Double-Digit Multiplication
3 – Mastery
• Multiplies the proper digit together.
• Basic multiplication is correct.
• "Carries" if necessary.
• Writes in a place holder.
• Lines up numbers properly.
• Adds products correctly.

Rubric
Double-Digit Multiplication
3 – Mastery
• Multiplies the proper digit together.
• Basic multiplication is correct.
• "Carries" if necessary.
• Writes in a place holder.
• Lines up numbers properly.
• Adds products correctly.

Rubric
Double-Digit Multiplication
3 – Mastery
• Multiplies the proper digit together.
• Basic multiplication is correct.
• "Carries" if necessary.
• Writes in a place holder.
• Lines up numbers properly.
• Adds products correctly.

Rubric
Double-Digit Multiplication
3 – Mastery
• Multiplies the proper digit together.
• Basic multiplication is correct.
• "Carries" if necessary.
• Writes in a place holder.
• Lines up numbers properly.
• Adds products correctly.

Rubric
Double-Digit Multiplication
3 – Mastery
• Multiplies the proper digit together.
• Basic multiplication is correct.
• "Carries" if necessary.
• Writes in a place holder.
• Lines up numbers properly.
• Adds products correctly.

Figure 37. Double-digit multiplication rubric showing student scores.

Figure 37 shows a few sample rubrics. From analyzing them, it is easy to see most students did not master being able to write in a place-holder or lining up numbers properly. With this information, the teacher can re-teach those skills in small groups as needed.

To clearly see the components children missed the most, you can create a spreadsheet. Mark the space if the child missed the component (does not have it highlighted). Then you have a visual record of the components missed. This process gives you a more accurate reading of what children missed versus looking at each completed rubric over and over again. This process can be used with different kind of tests. The students name will go down the vertical column and the item number from the test will go across the top, horizontally.

Student	Multi-plies proper digit	Basic math correct	Carries	Place holder	Lines up numbers	Adds products
#1				✓		
#2	✓				✓	
#3					✓	
#4				✓	✓	
#5				✓	✓	
#6		✓		✓	✓	
#7				✓	✓	

Figure 38. This spreadsheet allows you to quickly scroll down the columns to find the areas children (from Figure 37) will need to practice more before they can master the standard. Components children missed are checked off. In this case, many children will need to be re-taught "lining up numbers" and "using a place holder."

One way to determine the components of a rubric is to identify the steps or procedures laid out in the academic standard. Another way is to rephrase the language of the standard. Looking at California Academic Content Standards, Kindergarten, Measurement and Geometry 2.1, the first step is to understand the language of the standard. "Identify and describe common geometric objects (circle, triangle, square, rectangle, cube, sphere, and cone)."

As classroom teachers, we know that students can identify a shape without having the vocabulary to describe it, and alternatively, students may be able to describe a shape without being able to remember the proper name. Thus there must be two aspects or two rubrics for this standard, one to address "identifying" and one to address "describing" geometric objects.

Again, developing a common language is essential. In reference to this standard, "What defines describing a geometric shape?" To define a term, it may be necessary to look at the first grade standards. What will this first grade student need to know to be successful in coming years? In this case, a student must demonstrate mathematical vocabulary such as "faces/lack of faces, points (or corners)/lack of points, rolls/slides/spins, and be able to describe the difference between equal size faces on a cube versus rectangular faces and square faces on a rectangle."

Focusing on "identifying a geometric shape" in Figure 39, the 3, then must consist of the student being "...able to correctly identify at least seven of the nine common geometric shapes" (80% accuracy). "Describing a geometric shape," in Figure 40, the 3, then, must consist of the student being "...able to correctly name at least two attributes to describe six of the seven common geometric shapes." The finished rubrics look like Figure 39.

Measurement and Geometry 2.1

2.1 Identify and describe common geometric objects (e.g., circle, triangle, square, rectangle, cube, sphere, cone).

Identifies common geometric shapes

4 – Exemplary
All of "3" AND given one real life object for each of the nine geometric shapes.

3 – Mastery
The student is able to correctly identify at least seven of the nine common geometric shapes.

2 – Approaching
The student is able to correctly identify at least three of the nine common geometric shapes.

cont.

---

1 – Emerging
The student is able to identify at least one common geometric shapes.

0 – No Evidence
The student is not able to identify any geometric shapes.

Figure 39. A rubric that focuses on **identifying** common geometric shapes.

Although using a common language is an important part of understanding how to use and read rubrics, it's also important to understand how to fill out a rubric. We suggest using a highlighter to highlight each component so it's easily visible. Underlining or circling the components can sometimes be hard to see. Also, using a highlighter is fast in that you only have to make one quick mark across the component.

Measurement and Geometry 2.1

2.1 Identify and describe common geometric objects (e.g., circle, triangle, square, rectangle, cube, sphere, cone).

Describes common geometric shapes

4 – Exemplary
All of "3" AND given one real life object for each of the nine geometric shapes, and students can name three or more attributes.

3 – Mastery
The student is able to correctly name at least two attributes to describe each of the nine common shapes.

2 – Approaching
The student is able to correctly name at least one attribute for three or more common geometric shapes.

1 – Emerging
The student is only able to name attributes for two or fewer common geometric shape

0 – No Evidence
The student is not able to name any attributes of any common geometric shapes.

Figure 40. A rubric that focuses on **describing** common geometric shapes.

Each component of the rubric should be highlighted by the scorer to show where the child was demonstrating mastery and where he failed to meet mastery. Within a single paper or project, some components may be at the mastery level whereas some may be at the approaching level. There may even be some components that scored at the exemplary level. Remember that a student's work cannot receive a score of both exemplary and mastery for the same component. In Figure 41, a child cannot "include a variety of sentence types" (under the 4), and also have the same component highlighted under the 3, "includes some variety in sentence types." In the example in Figure 41, the shaded text in italics shows two of the same components shaded at different score levels, which is not correct. A child cannot score at the mastery level and the exemplary level in the same component. A good way to check to see if the correct amount of components has been shaded is to count how many components there are in one score level. In the example below, there are six components within each scoring level. Each component is worded appropriately for the different scoring levels. Count how many components have been shaded. Here there have been seven shaded so there has been one component shaded twice and will need to be corrected.

General Writing Rubric Grades 3-6

4 – Exemplary
- clearly addresses all parts of the writing task
- demonstrates a clear understanding of purpose
- maintains a consistent point of view, focus, and organizational structure, including paragraphing when appropriate
- includes a clearly presented central idea with relevant facts, details, and/or explanations
- *includes a variety of sentence types*
- contains zero errors in English language conventions (grammar, punctuation, capitalization, spelling)

3 – Mastery
- addresses all parts of the writing task
- demonstrates a general understanding of purpose

---

cont.

- maintains a mostly consistent point of view, focus, and organizational structure, including paragraphing when appropriate
- presents a central idea with mostly relevant facts, details, and/or explanations
- *includes some variety in sentence types*
- contains some errors in English language conventions (grammar, punctuation, capitalization, spelling). The errors do not interfere with the reader's understanding of the writing.

2 – Approaching
- addresses most parts of the writing task
- demonstrates some understanding of purpose
- maintains an inconsistent point of view, focus, and organizational structure, including paragraphing when appropriate
- suggests a central idea with limited facts, details, and/or explanations
- includes little variety in sentence types
- contains many errors in English language conventions (grammar, punctuation, capitalization, spelling). The errors interfere with the reader's understanding of the writing.

1 – Emerging
- addresses one part of the writing task
- demonstrates little understanding of purpose
- lacks a clear point of view, focus, and organizational structure, including paragraphing when appropriate
- lacks a central idea with most but may contain marginally related facts, details, and/or explanations
- includes no variety in sentence types
- contains serious errors in English language conventions (grammar, punctuation, capitalization, spelling). The errors interfere with the reader's understanding of the writing.

0 – No Evidence
- no paper turned in or incomplete
- paper cannot be read due to serious conventional errors, or does not make sense

Figure 41. Two of the same components are highlighted in two separate score levels, which is not correct.

However, a student could have exemplary "sentence types" but be "approaching" in "addresses all parts of the writing task." Those are two separate components scored in two separate score levels. See Figure 42.

General Writing Rubric Grades 3-6

4 – Exemplary
- clearly addresses all parts of the writing task
- demonstrates a clear understanding of purpose
- maintains a consistent point of view, focus, and organizational structure, including paragraphing when appropriate
- includes a clearly presented central idea with relevant facts, details, and/or explanations
- includes a variety of sentence types
- contains zero errors in English language conventions (grammar, punctuation, capitalization, spelling)

3 – Mastery
- addresses all parts of the writing task
- demonstrates a general understanding of purpose
- maintains a mostly consistent point of view, focus, and organizational structure, including paragraphing when appropriate
- presents a central idea with mostly relevant facts, details, and/or explanations
- includes some variety in sentence types
- contains some errors in English language conventions (grammar, punctuation, capitalization, spelling). The errors do not interfere with the reader's understanding of the writing.

2 – Approaching
- addresses most parts of the writing task
- demonstrates some understanding of purpose
- maintains an inconsistent point of view, focus, and organizational structure, including paragraphing when appropriate
- suggests a central idea with limited facts, details, and/or explanations
- includes little variety in sentence types
- contains many errors in English language conventions

---

cont.

(grammar, punctuation, capitalization, spelling). The errors interfere with the reader's understanding of the writing.

1 – Emerging
- addresses one part of the writing task
- demonstrates little understanding of purpose
- lacks a clear point of view, focus, and organizational structure, including paragraphing when appropriate
- lacks a central idea with most but may contain marginally related facts, details, and/or explanations
- includes no variety in sentence types
- contains serious errors in English language conventions (grammar, punctuation, capitalization, spelling). The errors interfere with the reader's understanding of the writing.

0 – No Evidence
- no paper turned in or incomplete
- paper cannot be read due to serious conventional errors, or does not make sense

Figure 42. General writing rubric, grades 3–6.

It is also possible and often necessary (depending on your academic standards) to break down some of the components even further. Some teachers say they would break down the standard identifying "sentence variety" down to specify "uses multiple complex sentences."

Altering Existing Rubrics

For many years, textbook companies have included assessments with their curriculum. In recent years, they have begun to include rubrics to match their assessments. A pre-written test designed by a textbook company may or may not match your state or school's academic standards or goals. If the assessment or task can accurately test your students' abilities to master your standards, use it. If the pre-written assessment matches a portion of your standards, take the pre-written assessment and modify it if necessary to ensure all components of the standard are addressed.

Many textbook publishers are now including general rubrics along with performance assessments of their units. These rubrics are intentionally vague and general, so they can be used with many different activities and across curricula despite varying academic expectations.

If you alter the assessment, chances are you will have to alter the rubric as well. To alter one of these rubrics to meet your standards (pun intended), you will need to combine the publisher's general components with the specific standards or goals that you, the teacher, are teaching and assessing. Likewise, if there is a concept or component in the pre-written rubric that you don't teach, or have not yet addressed, be sure you are not inadvertently assessing it and make sure it is taken out of the rubric.

---

3 – Mastery
- Student shows at least one way to solve a problem.
- Student uses at least one way to show thinking (diagrams, chart, formula, etc.)
- Student writes a clear explanation of how the problem was solved, including his or her thinking process

---

Figure 43. is a generalized math rubric that requires the following components to demonstrate mastery.

Let's say the specific standard you are addressing is for students to be able to demonstrate an understanding of perimeter and area using computation as well as another method of solving the problem. If you like the foundation of this rubric, but it doesn't quite have all the necessary components for your standard, revise it to include the necessary components. The revised mastery section for this rubric could read as shown in Figure 44.

---

3 – Mastery
- Student shows how to solve the problem using both computation and pictures/diagrams/charts.
- Computation is correct.
- Student writes a clear explanation of how the problem was solved, including his or her thinking process.

Figure 44. Generalized rubrics can be modified to suit the specific task.

The ability to express their thinking process is left untouched from the original rubric, because the ability to clarify and explain their thinking process not only codifies, internalizes, and solidifies a student's understanding of a process, it also gives you an insight into how their student heard and understood the instruction and how the student applies and generalizes knowledge.

Writing, in the past, has been left out of the subject of mathematics. But it is now being required in many schools because recent research shows that writing across the curriculum improves student success.

You will need to create many rubrics from scratch because a textbook may not include one. We do, however, advocate using rubrics that have already been created by textbook companies as long as the components measure what you are assessing or you have the ability to alter the rubric.

Checklists Are Not Rubrics

When looking at pre-written rubrics from textbooks or on the internet, be cautious. Many people will use the term "checklist" and "rubric" interchangeably, which is an incorrect use of the term "rubric" as we've defined it. They are two different tools.

A checklist can simply be a list of items to be completed on an assignment, but will not be used as a scoring tool. Or, a checklist can provide grading criteria for an assignment, which is made up of different items that are requirements of the assignment. These items are rated on a number scale, like the example in Figure 45. All you have to do is check off which number of points you believe each item is worth. Then, total up all points earned to get the final score (which is the total number of points earned out of the total possible).

Figure 45 is an example of a checklist. The components are listed, but there is no defining information to know which number of points a child has earned. The first component is how clearly defined the topic was. What is the difference between awarding a 4 and a 5? What is the difference between a 1 and a 5? What score is the grade level expectation? Is there a score for those who go above the grade level expectation? What if two teachers have completely different ideas on the definition of the numbers? Scoring will not be consistent from class to class.

Research Report Checklist

1. The topic of research was clearly defined.

    1   2   3   4   5

2. Concepts are accurately identified and clearly understood.

    1   2   3   4   5

3. The information researched addressed a problem.

    1   2   3   4   5

4. The information researched addressed alternatives for solution.

    1   2   3   4   5

5. The information researched addressed the best solution.

    1   2   3   4   5

6. The end product has some kind of visual aspect.

    1   2   3   4   5

7. The student demonstrated understanding of topic during small group discussion.

    1   2   3   4   5

Total Points Possible: 35 points

Total Points Earned:_____

Figure 45. To score a task using a checklist, the numbers are circled then added up for a point total. The numbers are circled based on the ability level the teacher feels the student demonstrated.

The second problem with using checklists as scoring tools is that all components are basically worth five points each. Is clearly defining the topic (component one) as difficult as "re-searching information for the best solution" (component five)? Once you compute the score, you end up with a number, which almost always is computed into a percentage, which we associ-ate with letter grades. The checklist below is worth 35 points. If a student gets a total of 30 points out of 35, this equals an 86% or a B, yet we don't have any clarifying information as to how each score was determined. This goes against the philosophy of rubrics. Rubrics are to provide specific information about how a child has performed on a task. A checklist lacks this information that a rubric provides, so we strongly suggest not using them unless they can be modified into a rubric to include score levels with descriptive components.

Discussion Questions

1. What unifying academic standards does your school use? Do all teachers and administrators interpret each standard the same way? Explain.

2. What reference tool does your staff use to aid in "unpacking" or "decoding" standards, and how does that aid in creating and interpreting assessments?

3. Does your school have a common language for looking at stu-dent work? Do all staff members agree on what "passing" or "mastery" looks like across grade levels?

4. Does your school community have a shared understanding of various levels of accomplishment? How did your school reach this shared understanding, or how could your staff begin to build a shared understanding student accomplishment?

5. Create a five-point (0, 1, 2, 3, 4) writing rubric for the following selection of standards and assignment:

Virginia Writing Standards—Third Grade

3.9   The student will write descriptive paragraphs.
   e)   Develop a plan for writing.
   f)   Focus on a central idea.
   g)   Group related ideas.
   h)   Include descriptive details that elaborate the central idea.

Have you ever taken a family vacation? Write a three-paragraph essay that tells the story of that vacation. Include how your vacation started, what made that vacation memorable, and how it ended. Brainstorm on the attached paper before you start writing.

Involvement

◈

First Steps: Getting Students On Board

If schools are making a transition from using traditional letter grades to using rubrics and giving rubric scores, teachers will need to take time to introduce rubrics to students and explain how they will be implemented in the classroom. So many times teachers give rubrics to children, but don't explain exactly what they are and how to use them to help them with a given task.

Let students know that the reason for using this grading system is to help them; not simply for a grade to put on a report card. Using different language, we have told students from kindergarten through adulthood, "Rubrics set you up for success because they tell you exactly what you need to do on an assignment and how well you need to complete it. Before turning in an assignment, when you review the rubric, you may find you are missing parts of the assignment or did not complete some parts as well as you should have. This gives you a chance to go back and fix any mistakes to achieve a better score. If the mistakes are not fixed, you will have a good idea of the score you might receive since the rubric points out below grade level work as well. Finally, once the rubric is filled in, it shows you specifically how well you completed the assignment. This lets us know what your strengths are and also what you need to work on."

This first step to implementing rubrics with students is to have a discussion about the grading process. A teacher may use the following approach:

1. Explain what standards are.

"Standards are another way of telling you all the wonderful things you will learn each year. I may write standards on the board, have them posted on the walls, or you may see them written on your papers. This is an easy way to let everyone know what you are learning. Here is an example of a standard." Examples, especially for upper grade students, should be shown on an overhead projector so children know what they look like. Figure 46 provides an example of a fourth grade standard from Ohio.

Ohio Academic Content Standards (grade 4)

Number and Number Systems

1. Identify and generate equivalent forms of fractions and decimals. For example:
   a. Connect physical, verbal, and symbolic representations of fractions, decimals, and whole numbers; e.g., ½, 5/10, "five tenths," 0.5, shaded rectangles with half, and five tenths.
   b. Understand and explain that ten tenths is the same as one whole in both fraction and decimal form.

Figure 46. An example of an Ohio standard.

2. Have an example of a task or assessment that was created based on a particular standard and use it to take the class through the scoring process.

"Here is an example of an assessment you might have. Notice this assessment was written from the standard I just showed you." Explain the assessment to the class being sure to point out the directions or items that are most important or heavily weighted, which will be the components of the rubric.

Equivalent forms of fractions and decimals

Number and Number Systems Standard 1

Create shaded figures to show the following as fractions and decimals. Have a written explanation to explain each picture and your understanding of equivalent fractions and decimals.

½   5/10   10/10

Figure 47. Equivalent forms of fractions and decimals.

3. Explain when the assessment is graded, students will get a rubric.

"To score your assessment you will get a piece of paper that tells you all the things you did well on and all the things you will need more practice on. This piece of paper is called a rubric. Before you complete an assessment, you will get a copy of the rubric so you know you will be scored on. It can help guide you on how to best complete the assessment. When you get the assessment back after I've graded it using the rubric, the rubric will let you know your score." Have an example of a rubric that goes with the assessment to show on an overhead projector.

Number and Number Systems Standard 1
Equivalent Forms of Fractions and Decimals

4 – Exemplary
- Uses more than the three required fractions to find equivalent forms of fractions and decimals
- Math is correct with no mistakes. Different ways to find answer may be used.
- Written explanation demonstrates depth and understanding of equivalent forms of fractions and decimals

3 – Mastery
- Uses at least the three required fractions to find equivalent forms of fractions and decimals
- Math may have one or two mistakes
- Written explanation demonstrates a general understanding of equivalent forms of fractions and decimals

2 – Approaching
- Uses less than the three required fractions to find equivalent forms of fractions and decimals
- Math may have more than two mistakes
- Written explanation demonstrates little understanding of equivalent forms of fractions and decimals

1 – Emerging
- No shaded figures used to show equivalents
- Math is incorrect
- No written explanation

---

cont.

0– No Evidence
  - Assignment is incomplete
  - Assignment is not turned in
  - Assignment does not address equivalent forms of fractions and decimals

Figure 48. Fractions and decimals rubric.

4. Explain the rubric.

Explain the overall layout: the score levels, the qualifying terms, and the components. Start with "mastery" since this is the "passing" score. "If you do a good job on your assessment and complete all the parts correctly, you will get a score of 3. This is called "mastery." To get a 3, you would have to have all these components completed correctly." We expect all students to master the standard being assessed. It's very important for students to know what is expected of them to demonstrate mastery of a particular skill. Before children are taught how to identify mastery work as well as work not at the mastery level, they have to learn what the definition of mastery is.

Using a rubric, like the one mentioned in the previous section, to provide a definition for mastery as well as the other qualifying terms is a good place to start. It's necessary to continuously examine student work with the class to show them what qualifies for mastery and what does not. Before students start to self-reflect on their work or the work of their classmates (for purposes of peer editing), they have to be able to identify what mastery level work looks like. All children in the class need to have the same understanding of what mastery level work looks like.

Show the class the components of the mastery level of this rubric and explain what each one means. Then explain the rest of the score levels starting with the approaching level (2), then the emerging level (1), no evidence (0), and finally, the exemplary level (4). Reiterate the goal is to score at least a 3. Although it would be nice for all children to score a 4, that is reserved only for those who go significantly above and beyond the grade level expectation.

When introducing the rubric, explain it will always be presented at the same time the task is assigned. By going over the rubric, students will know what they will need to do to complete the task and what help (if any) he or she will need. Students can ask clarifying questions if they do not understand the different components of the rubric.

It is good teaching practice to encourage students to ask questions. When students are aware of the expectation, it makes it easier for them to meet that expectation. When given the option, students nearly always say they will "shoot for the 3 or 4." Rubrics show students the steps necessary to meet their goal.

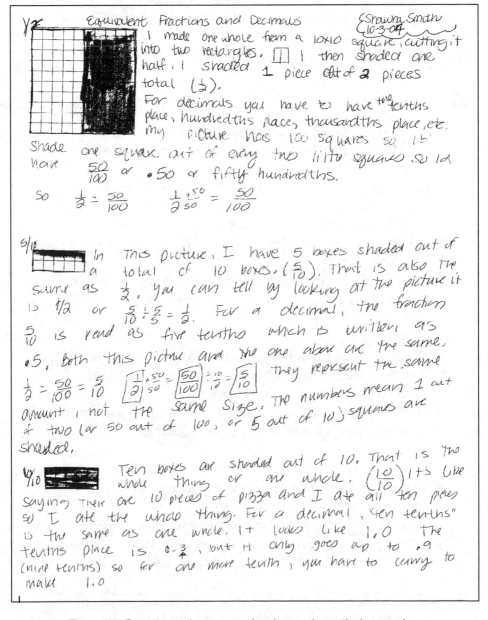

Figure 49. Sample student paper showing mathematical reasoning.

5. Show the completed assessment with the rubric once it has been filled out.

"Here is an example of a completed assessment. Let's look at it to see if we agree with the score given on the rubric." Put the assessment on the overhead projector and review it with the class. Then put the rubric on the overhead projector to show the class how the assessment was scored.

Explain that the highlighted components are the items this student's paper demonstrated. Each different component can be highlighted in different score levels depending on how the student completed the assessment. Show how overall score was awarded as well.

**Number and Number Systems Standard 1
Equivalent Forms of Fractions and Decimals**

4 – Exemplary   Overall Score ___3___
* Uses more than the three required fractions to find equivalent forms of fractions and decimals
* Math is correct with no mistakes. Different ways to find answer may be used.
* Written explanation demonstrates depth and understanding of equivalent forms of fractions and decimals

3 – Mastery
* Uses at least the three required fractions to find equivalent forms of fractions and decimals
* Math may have one or two mistakes
* Written explanation demonstrates a general understanding of equivalent forms of fractions and decimals

2 – Approaching
* Uses less than the three required fractions to find equivalent forms of fractions and decimals
* Math may have more than two mistakes
* Written explanation demonstrates little understanding of equivalent forms of fractions and decimals

---

cont.

1 – Emerging
  • No shaded figures used to show equivalents
  • Math is incorrect
  • No written explanation

0 – No Evidence
  • Assignment is incomplete
  • Assignment is not turned in
  • Assignment does not address equivalent forms of fractions and decimals

Figure 50. Fractions and decimals rubric.

After students understand the process, they can have a chance at scoring an assignment. Have another assignment to share with the class on the overhead projector. The example in Figure 51 is a basic writing task based on the "Six Traits of Writing" handbook (http://www.nwrel.org/assessment/department.asp?d=1). Figure 51 is a general lesson that could fit any state's writing standards. The focus of this task was word choice, which the rubric reflects.

The day the cat ate my Mom's car

My mom was in a rush. Her short blond hair was blowing in the breeze and her shoes snapped on the driveway as she ran for the car. She wasn't listening as I yelled for our cat, Barney.

"Mom," I cried, "Mom, I can't find Barney anywhere."

"It's Ok," she yelled over her shoulder, "He's a CAT. He's fine. We're going to be late for your teacher conference!"

I knew my mom was right, so I dragged myself to the backseat of the car. I hauled open the door and threw my backpack inside, narrowly missing…Barney!

"Mom," I yelled, "I found Barney!"

cont.

"That's nice, dear." She said as she backed the car out of the driveway and into the busy street.

"No, mom, he's here, in the car."

But mom wasn't listening to me, she was busy peeking both ways at the stop sign.

Figure 51. Writing sample for class discussion.

To keep the class engaged, we give each student a copy of the rubric and a highlighter so they can also score the paper as the instructor models.

To begin the lesson, the instructor puts the transparency on the overhead projector and starts by saying "This is an example of a student's story/journal entry/essay. No one in this class wrote it. When I look at this writing the first thing I notice is that this student put a title. Is this title interesting? Does it grab you? The day the cat ate my Mom's car is more interesting than My Cat. I think that's a good title. Let's check that rubric." The instructor replaces the writing sample with a transparency of the writing rubric that the class has been using, and highlights the appropriate phrase.

Word Choice Rubric

4 – Exemplary
- Words are powerful and interesting
- The reader can make a picture in their head of exactly what the writer is trying to show.
- The reader can tell that the writer chose extraordinary words
- The title is intriguing

3 – Mastery
- Words are chosen and used appropriately
- It is easy to figure out what the writer intended

cont.

- The reader can tell that the writer used words that they use everyday
- The title fits the essay

2 – Approaching
- Writer demonstrates a limited vocabulary or the words don't make sense
- It is hard to figure out what the writer is trying to say
- The writer uses a lot of clichés or repeats him/herself
- The title does not fit the essay

1 – Emerging
- There is little or no writing turned in
- The writer plagiarized someone else's work
- There is a very limited meaning coming through
- No title is given

Figure 52. The first component is highlighted. There is no order in which you need to shade the components. The title was one of the first things to read and it was known to be a component since you reviewed the rubric before scoring the paper.

"The next thing I notice is that I have a hard time reading this handwriting. Even though handwriting is not on this rubric, it makes it hard to figure out what the author is trying to say. I might miss some good word choices if I can't read this handwriting. And it might make someone just skip it, and not read it at all. However, let's start reading."

As the teacher reads the essay out loud to the class, doing a "think aloud," pausing to point out positives, like descriptive words, or negatives, like missing punctuation or indecipherable words, he or she keeps referring back to the rubric, highlighting when appropriate, or modeling "Oh, too bad, this person forgot to check to see if their word choice made sense."

Word Choice

4   Exemplary
  - Words are powerful and interesting
  - The reader can make a picture in their head of exactly what the writer is trying to show.
  - The reader can tell that the writer chose extraordinary words
  - The title is intriguing

3   Mastery
  - Words are chosen and used appropriately
  - It is easy to figure out what the writer intended
  - The reader can tell that the writer used words that they use everyday
  - The title fits the essay

2   Approaching
  - Writer demonstrates a limited vocabulary or the words don't make sense
  - It is hard to figure out what the writer is trying to say
  - The writer uses a lot of clichés or repeats him/herself
  - The title does not fit the essay

1   Emerging
  - There is little or no writing turned in
  - The writer plagiarized someone else's work
  - There is a very limited meaning coming through
  - No title is given

Figure 53. The next component is highlighted.

"Hmmm, I see that some of the words are extraordinary. I can tell that this writer really stretched himself. That's in the 4 but they also used words that didn't make sense sometimes. That's in the 2 category. I see that this person used creative words and made a picture in my mind, and that this story had a beginning, middle, and end. It was clear to me who the main characters were, what the problem was, and what the solution was.

Word Choice

4 – Exemplary   Overall Score   _3_

- Words are powerful and interesting
- The reader can make a picture in their head of exactly what the writer is trying to show.
- The reader can tell that the writer chose extraordinary words
- *The title is intriguing*

3 – Mastery

- *Words are chosen and used appropriately*
- It is easy to figure out what the writer intended
- *The reader can tell that the writer used words that they use everyday*
- The title fits the essay

2 – Approaching

- Writer demonstrates a limited vocabulary or the words don't make sense
- *It is hard to figure out what the writer is trying to say*
- The writer uses a lot of clichés or repeats him/herself
- The title does not fit the essay

1 – Emerging

- There is little or no writing turned in
- The writer plagiarized someone else's work
- There is a very limited meaning coming through
- No title is given

Figure 54. The final components are highlighted and an overall score is given.

When the teacher is done reading and commenting on the essay, he or she can then refer back to the rubric. The overall score is that which contains the majority of highlighting. Again, the teacher will need to model compromise. It looks to me like this person had more highlights in the 3 than in any other category."

We used "thumbs up/thumbs down" to demonstrate agreement or disagreement without creating cacophony in the classroom, and allowing the instructor to call on select individuals to voice their rationale for agreement or disagreement.

For a variety of examples, we saved work samples from previous classes (always remembering to remove any names from assignments we shared with students). It helps students to see what their peers have accomplished. As a whole class, you can look at the assignment and rubric together and model for the children how to fill out the rubric and score an assignment appropriately.

As students practice using rubrics, the teacher can begin to offer more difficult samples to score, refining the students' critical thinking skills. It is of course easier to identify a "does not meet standard" than it is to distinguish between a "mastery" and "exemplary" sample. After recreating this lesson several times, and with revisiting when new elements were to be scored, we began scoring several writing samples at a time with the class, making sure to include an "exemplary" sample and often an "approaching" or "emerging" sample as well.

For students to be able to use rubrics, they need to have a discriminating eye. With upper primary or more mature students, teachers can have the students trade papers blindly (no student name or identifying mark) and score each other's papers using teacher created rubrics. They don't have to always practice using rubrics as a whole class with the teacher in front of the overhead.

There are a few ways to have students evaluate each other's work. First, children can use rubrics and simply highlight the components they feel the work qualifies as. You can tell them that they are the reviewers and they will have to score the work (based on the quality of the work, not if they like the person whose work they are scoring!). Again, it's important to point out this is not necessarily going to be the student's final score as you, the teacher, have the final say.

This process will not be completed in one day. It will take a few days to introduce rubrics and a few months to review and fully understand how they work. When students are comfortable with rubrics, let them fill out a rubric for their own assignments. It is a good way for them to check over their own work before they turn the assignment in to the teacher for the final scoring. Of course, they need to know the components they high light and the overall score they award themselves may not be the final score they receive from the teacher.

After using rubrics with students, they will begin to see how much better rubrics are than traditional letter grades because of the built-in quality feedback. Students want to succeed and rubrics set them up for success.

Involving Students

Rubrics are usually written by the classroom teacher, a team of teachers, or are designed together by the students and teacher. But when the students are involved in how they are assessed, they have ownership of the task and they also feel more responsible for completing their work to the best of their ability. So how can students take part in designing rubrics?

We feel that it is essential that all students eventually take ownership of rubrics by helping to develop the rubrics that they will be scored with. Our experience has been that students are more successful when they internalize the task and scoring tool by helping to design it. Initially, students can use a pre-written rubric to score their own or each other's assignments, developing a facility with the scoring tool.

Having students take responsibility and ownership of their own learning by coming to consensus on student-created rubrics is a process not a goal. When students have developed a familiarity with reading rubrics, being scored with rubrics and being able to explain not only why they received a particular score but also what they as an individual need to do to improve their score, teachers can only then begin to have students create their own rubrics. Creating rubrics as a class assumes that students are familiar with consensus building and compromise. If you are working with a population that has never had the opportunity to build consensus or had to compromise for the good of the group, the project of creating rubrics must take a back seat to creating a sense of safe community, respect, and risk-taking within your classroom.

When writing rubrics with students, it's important that students have an understanding of what a scoring rubric is and how to use one. Students also need to have a clear understanding of what "mastery" is (i.e., what the instructor's expectations are for each student). To establish our expectations of mastery, we use an overhead projector and already completed rubrics and tasks like the writing sample used in the previous chapter.

We never used writing samples from our own class, choosing to "borrow" anonymous samples from other classrooms, from textbooks, or from the "Six Traits of Writing" handbooks. (http://www.nwrel.org/assessment/department.asp?d=1). Using writing from your own classroom opens up an individual student to praise, but also to damage to their self-esteem, since the instructor uses this writing sample to publicly point out what meets expectations, but also what is not up to expectations and needs to be improved.

Writing Rubrics With Students

Before writing a rubric with the class, the instructor must have a clear vision of what his or her academic expectations are. The instructor should also have a clear vision of what the goals of the lesson are. Because you are the instructor, you are responsible for teaching and assessing certain skills or facts. This means that the students do not retain complete control over the rubric. You do. As the instructor, you are teaching students to design an appropriate rubric, not giving over control of the material. The instructor should have a goal in mind (i.e., to demonstrate mastery, a student must...). We have found that students tend to be much harder on themselves and each other than teachers tend to be! Students tend to be much more specific than global, and they tend to be much stricter about requirements for each score. Part of your task, as an educator is to teach the students an appreciation for a diversity and range of work.

When creating a rubric with a group, initially the instructor needs to clarify the end product for the group. After being scored with rubrics and manipulating rubrics themselves, they should be familiar with your expectations, and the expectations of the standards or the curriculum. As the students brainstorm what the rubric should entail, write their ideas down on chart paper, the board, or on an overhead so that all the students can see all the ideas. After you have taken all the suggestions, narrow the rubric down to no more than five components per score level. Have the students work in pairs or small groups (if age appropriate) to examine the rubric, combine ideas, or add ideas. When the rubric is complete, type it and distribute it to each student so as they work on the project they can refer back to the scoring guide.

This process, like many things we do with children, will be time consuming when you first start. After they have practiced this skill, students will know what your goal is and what components are necessary to be assessed. Again, it is an essential aspect of developing critical thinking and self-motivation to give students the ability to score themselves.

The following is an area and perimeter assignment from a fourth grade class. When generating a rubric with the students, it's important to go through a series of steps to ensure the rubric is measuring the goal you, the teacher, have in mind.

1. Let students know what standards or goals the assignment will address.

The assignment in Figure 55 will address California Measurement & Geometry Standards 1.1 and 1.4 (two out of the four standards). Students need to know the standard because when they help create the components, they will have to refer to the standard so they know exactly what skill they are to demonstrate.

Area and Perimeter Standards (California, 4th grade)

1.1 Measure the area of rectangular shapes by using appropriate units, square centimeter (cm^2), square meter (m^2), square kilometer (km^2), square inches (in^2), square yard (yd^2), square mile (mi^2).

1.2 Recognize that rectangles that have the same area can have different perimeters.

1.3 Understand that rectangles that have the same perimeter can have different areas.

1.4 Understand and use formulas to solve problems involving perimeters and areas of rectangles and squares. Use these formulas to find the areas of more complex figures by dividing the figures into basic shapes. (California State Academic Standards Frameworks)

Figure 55. Area and perimeter standards including sub-standards that will be taught and assessed for this particular task.

2. Hand out and review the assignment with the sutdents.

They will need to know the activities necessary to complete the assignment. This is one of many activities created to teach area and perimeter, which is reflective of the final assessment. Remember all lesson plans should include assignments and activities that prepare students for taking the final assessment which should be created before any teaching takes place to ensure the lessons planned are geared toward the final assessment of the standard(s) being taught.

Assignment

Show the area and perimeter of at least two different shapes any way you know how. Cut out the shapes from graph paper and glue the shapes down on a large sheet of paper. Show how you got the area and perimeter of the shapes using numbers and written explanations.

Measurement & Geometry Standards 1.1, 1.4

Figure 56. Sample M&G assignment.

In class, students had previously learned and practiced three different ways of finding the perimeter and the area.

Perimeter

- Count (and label) each side all around the figure
- Count the lengths of the sides and add the total lengths of each side
- Formula (for regular rectangular shapes): $P = 2$ multiply $(l + w)$

Area

- Counting (and labeling) each square
- Break up the figure into squares/rectangles and use the formula to find the area of each figure then add them together
- Formula (for regular rectangular shapes): $A = l$ multiply w

3. Ask the students what things I, as their teacher, would expect them to be able to do to complete this assignment at the 4th grade level.

In partnerships or groups, let the students come up with no more than five components of the assignment they would need to complete to receive a good score (mastery level). More than five components may be too many (depending on the assignment) to keep track of when scoring the assignment.

When creating a rubric, remember to start with the mastery level (what you would expect the child to be able to do to complete the assignment at grade level). Then from there you create the components for the other point values (approaching, emerging, no evidence, exemplary). Remind the children to look at the standards and the assignment. The components they come up with should be the most important as it relates to those two documents. They can be vague since you will discuss the degree of the components for the other point values later.

4. List all the ideas from each group on the overhead projector.

A lot of students will come up with the same components. You'll also find the students tend to be more specific than you would. Remind them you're looking for the most important components in relation to the standards and the assignment that should be required for mastery.

Measurement & Geometry Standards 1.1, 1.4

- Neatness
- Correct math (no mistakes)
- Uses correct units
- Has name, date, and assignment on the paper
- Uses formulas for area and perimeter
- Has to have two different shapes to find the area and perimeter
- Math can have some mistakes
- Written explanation show you understand area and perimeter
- Spelling and grammar are correct in written explanation
- Paper is colorful

Figure 57. Possible components students may want to include in the rubric.

Notice one student said one component should be for math to be "...correct with no mistakes" while another student suggested the "math can have some mistakes." Put up both suggestions so that there are different options for students to vote on.

5. Vote for no more than five overall components.

As the teacher, you know what you want the end rubric to look like. Go through the different components the children came up with and discuss why a component may or may not be appropriate to put on the rubric before voting. For the component dealing with math mistakes, it's important for you, as the teacher, to think about what is usually required for mastery level. If you require 100% correctness, it may be wise to have the component read "math has to be correct with no mistakes." If you require 90% correctness, it may be okay to allow for a few mistakes. Also consider what the assignment's main goal is. Is it to have basic math correct? Is it to use the formulas for area and perimeter correct? If the focus is not basic math, a few mistakes may be okay, and still show the student has mastered the particular standard(s).

All teachers have different methods for taking a whole class vote. Any method your students are familiar with is appropriate.

6. Once you get your components, start filling out the rubric.

These first components, like discussed before, are the components for the mastery level (score of 3). From there you, with the students or on your own (to save time), can fill in the rest of the components for the different score levels. If your time is running out you can finish creating the rubric because the students helped to create the important piece, which is the mastery section.

7. Fill in the different components for the different score levels (if doing this with the whole class).

If students are creating this portion of the rubric with you, have them understand this part is fairly simple since they have the basic components already. All they have to do is modify the sentence of the component at the mastery level with defining words like "all," "most," "some," "none," and so on. Of course some components will have more thoughtful rephrasing depending on what the component is.

Area & Perimeter 1.1 and 1.4

4 - Exemplary

3 - Mastery
- Uses appropriate units with one or two mistakes (Standard 1.1)
- Uses formulas with one or two mistakes (Standard 1.4)
- Uses at least two shapes to find the area and perimeter
- Math may have one or two mistakes
- Written explanation demonstrates a general understanding of area and perimeter

2 - Approaching

1 – Emerging

0– No Evidence

Figure 58. How to start creating a rubric by deciding on the components of the mastery section first.

8. Review the rubric as a whole to make sure it is attainable, it makes sense in relation to the standards and the assignment, and all components are worded properly.

If the exemplary section says, "Student uses more than three ways..." make sure the mastery level doesn't repeat the same component. An acceptable wording for the mastery level could be, "Student uses at least two ways..."

9. Type up the final rubric.

Area & Perimeter 1.1 and 1.4

4 – Exemplary
- Uses appropriate units with no mistakes (Standard 1.1)
- Uses formulas with no mistakes (Standard 1.4)
- Uses more than two shapes to find the area and perimeter
- Math is correct with no mistakes. Different ways to find answer may be used.
- Written explanation demonstrates depth and understanding of area and perimeter

3 – Mastery
- Uses appropriate units with one or two mistakes (Standard 1.1)
- Uses formulas with one or two mistakes (Standard 1.4)
- Uses at least two shapes to find the area and perimeter
- Math may have one or two mistakes
- Written explanation demonstrates a general understanding of area and perimeter

2 – Approaching
- Does not use appropriate units (Standard 1.1)
- Does not use formulas properly (Standard 1.4)
- Uses less than two shapes to find the area and perimeter
- Math may have more than two mistakes
- Written explanation demonstrates little understanding of area and perimeter

1 – Emerging
- Does not attempt to use units (Standard 1.1)
- Does not attempt to use formulas (Standard 1.4)
- No shapes used to find area and perimeter
- Math is incorrect
- No written explanation

0 – No Evidence
- Assignment is incomplete
- Assignment is not turned in
- Assignment does not address area or perimeter

Figure 59. Final rubric.

Although many students are skilled typists, it is a good idea for you to type the rubric yourself to make sure all wording is correct.

10. Hand out the final rubric the next day and review it with the students.

Students will be pleased to see the completed rubric. They will feel proud that they helped create the very tool with which they will be graded. It helps them to take ownership of the task and encourages them to do a good job on the assignment because they helped decide how they should be scored.

If there are multiple standards being scored on one rubric, be sure to award each individual standard a separate score as well as an overall score. On the student sample below, each rubric component is labeled with the separate standards (that apply) so it's easy to see what score will be received. The overall score is awarded from the rubric as a whole. For example, on the student sample below, she scored a 4 for Measurement & Geometry Standard 1.1, and a 4 for Measurement & Geometry Standard 1.4. Overall, she scored a 4 because she had more components highlighted at the exemplary than any other level and she went above because she exceeded the expectation as noted on the rubric.

Area & Perimeter 1.1 and 1.4

4 – Exemplary
- Uses appropriate units with no mistakes (Standard 1.1)
- Uses formulas with no mistakes (Standard 1.4)
- Uses more than two shapes to find the area and perimeter
- Math is correct with no mistakes. Different ways to find answer may be used.
- Written explanation demonstrates depth and understanding of area and perimeter

3 – Mastery
- Uses appropriate units with one or two mistakes (Standard 1.1)

---

cont.

- Uses formulas with one or two mistakes (Standard 1.4)
- Uses at least two shapes to find the area and perimeter
- Math may have one or two mistakes
- Written explanation demonstrates a general understanding of area and perimeter

2 – Approaching
- Does not use appropriate units (Standard 1.1)
- Does not use formulas properly (Standard 1.4)
- Uses less than two shapes to find the area and perimeter
- Math may have more than two mistakes
- Written explanation demonstrates little understanding of area and perimeter

1 – Emerging
- Does not attempt to use units (Standard 1.1)
- Does not attempt to use formulas (Standard 1.4)
- No shapes used to find area and perimeter
- Math is incorrect
- No written explanation

0 – No Evidence
- Assignment is incomplete
- Assignment is not turned in
- Assignment does not address area or perimeter

Figure 60. Completed rubric scored with the class, based on the student example in Figure 61 on pages 106 and 107.

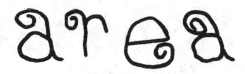

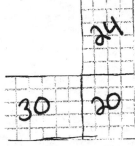

$$+ \begin{array}{r} 30 \\ 24 \\ + 20 \\ \hline 74 \end{array}$$

A = 74 sq. units.

I found this answer by dividing the shape in three sections. I used the area equals length x width formula for the rectangles made in the shape. Then, after I found the total of each rectangle, I added them together. My answer is 74 sq. units

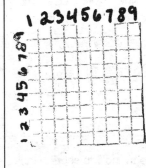

I found this area out by counting all of the squares. I counted 28 squares. My total is 28 square units.

A = L x W
A = 9 x 9
A = 81

To figure this problem out I using the area equals length times width formula. I timsed 9x9 and came up with 81 square units. 81 square units is my answer.

cont.

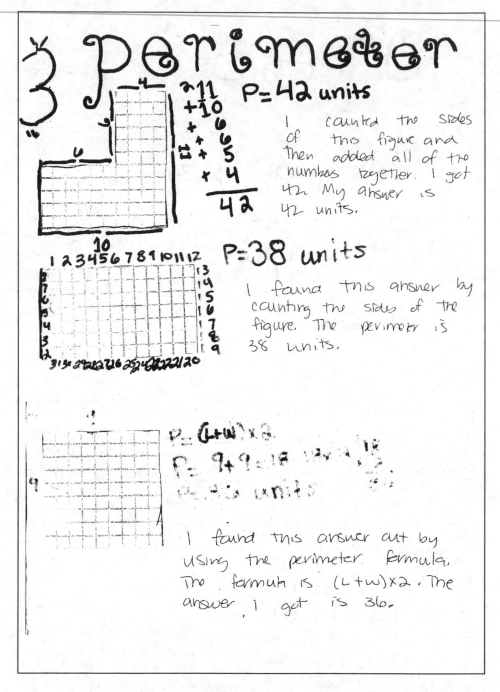

3 "u" perimeter

$P = 42$ units

$$\begin{array}{r} 11 \\ + 10 \\ + 6 \\ + 6 \\ + 5 \\ + 4 \\ \hline 42 \end{array}$$

I counted the sides of this figure and then added all of the numbers together. I got 42. My answer is 42 units.

$P = 38$ units

I found this answer by counting the sides of the figure. The perimeter is 38 units.

$P = (L + W) \times 2$
$P = 9 + 9 = 18$ ...
... units ...

I found this answer out by using the perimeter formula. The formula is $(L + W) \times 2$. The answer I got is 36.

Figure 61. This student example was used to help a class learn how to score a task using a rubric.

How Do Middle and High School Fit Into This Theory?

Teachers we've spoken with who teach at the higher levels tell us that using this model of assessment design and rubric scoring is not realistic for their level. The reasons they most commonly give are:

- We have 120–150 students.

- Colleges want letter grades.

- It takes too much instructional time and we only get 40–50 minutes with our students each day.

- There is so much curriculum to cover that we barely have time to do that, let alone have the kids help us develop rubrics.

- If we let our students score themselves, they would always give themselves the best score even if they know they didn't deserve it.

We propose that rubrics actually help to solve many problems with middle and high school grading. Using teacher-designed rubrics actually saves teacher preparation time. Students at both the elementary and secondary level benefit from helping to design rubrics because it clarifies the assignment for them and lets them take ownership.

When a middle or high school teacher hands out the assignment, he or she must hand out the rubric with it. Teachers should be taking the time to go over the assignment, so spend a few more minutes to let the students know how they will be evaluated. The students then have the assignment and they know exactly how they will be scored. That alone will save class time usually spent discussing grades, because students at this level are always concerned with how they will be scored.

We also believe using rubrics with middle and high school students will help the teacher to stay focused when scoring so many papers. When faced with 130 papers to score, it is easy to lose perspective after grading 50 papers. A rubric forces the assessor to stay focused and allows him to only highlight the components demonstrated in the assignment because the components are what the students are being scored on. There does not have to be a lot of extra time spent making notes in the margins because the student's spelling is atrocious. If that is a component on your rubric, it gets highlighted one time and that lets the student know spelling is an area to work on. Of course, there may still be times when the teacher will make written comments for the students, but overall, a rubric should address most issues.

We encourage students to take a rubric and score themselves before they hand in their paper so they can reflect on their work. Students could take this opportunity to revise their work to potentially improve their score. They need to know what ever they score themselves is not necessarily the same score you will award them. Most of the time, students are very honest and sometimes harder on themselves than an instructor might be. It may also allow them to recognize what areas they need your help with so they can make improvements.

The only difficulty we foresee with using rubric scores at the high school level may be college admissions. Colleges have always used grade point average (GPA) as part of college admission applications. However, the academic goal is for students, teachers, and parents to be more informed about the grading process and what strengths and weaknesses the student has—even at the high school level. Many quality college admissions processes weigh the student's writing samples and personal letters of recommendation more heavily than they do a student's GPA or class standing.

Photo Copying

Once you and your students have worked together to create a rubric, it must be useful and manageable. If you are starting with a completed rubric, or you are introducing the rubric to a group, use an overhead projector so that it can be seen by all of the students. Common sense dictates that you use a dark font that is large enough and clear enough to be seen clearly by everyone in the room. Fancy, curly fonts distract students and keep them from focusing on the content. You may want to give students individual copies of the rubric so they can make notes as the discussion about the assignment and rubric progresses.

When using rubrics, it is useful to shrink the rubric down and copy four to one $8^{1}/_{2}$ x 11 piece of paper. This helps to avoid wasting paper. For a class of 32 children, eight pieces of paper will be used to make 32 rubrics instead of 32 pieces of paper.

4th Grade Writing Rubric

Exemplary
-clearly addresses all parts of the writing task
-demonstrates a clear understanding of purpose
-maintains a consistent point of view, focus, and organizational structure, including paragraphing when appropriate
-includes a clearly presented central idea with relevant facts, details, and/or explanations
-includes a variety of sentence types
-contains few, if any, errors in the conventions of the English language (grammar, punctuation, capitalization, spelling). These errors do not interfere with the reader's understanding of the writing.

Mastery
-addresses all parts of the writing task
-demonstrates a general understanding of purpose
-maintains a mostly consistent point of view, focus, and organizational structure, including paragraphing when appropriate
-presents a central idea with mostly relevant facts, details, and/or explanations
-includes a variety of sentence types
-contains some errors in the conventions of the English language (grammar, punctuation, capitalization, spelling). These errors do not interfere with the reader's understanding of the writing.

Emerging
-addresses only parts of the writing tasks
-demonstrates little understanding of purpose
-maintains an inconsistent point of view, focus, and/or organizational structure
-suggests a central idea with limited facts, details, and/or explanations
-includes little variety in sentence types
-contains several errors in the conventions of the English language (grammar, punctuation, capitalization, spelling). These errors may interfere with the reader's understanding of the writing.

No Evidence
-addresses only one part of the writing task
-demonstrates no understanding of purpose
-lacks a clear point of view, focus, and/or organizational structure
-lacks a central idea but may contain marginally related facts, details, and/or explanations
-includes no sentence variety
-contains serious errors in the conventions of the English language (grammar, punctuation, capitalization, spelling). These errors interfere with the reader's understanding of the writing.

4th Grade Writing Rubric

4 **Exemplary**
-clearly addresses all parts of the writing task
-demonstrates a clear understanding of purpose
-maintains a consistent point of view, focus, and organizational structure, including paragraphing when appropriate
-includes a clearly presented central idea with relevant facts, details, and/or explanations
-includes a variety of sentence types
-contains few, if any, errors in the conventions of the English language (grammar, punctuation, capitalization, spelling). These errors do not interfere with the reader's understanding of the writing.

3 **Mastery**
-addresses all parts of the writing task
-demonstrates a general understanding of purpose
-maintains a mostly consistent point of view, focus, and organizational structure, including paragraphing when appropriate
-presents a central idea with mostly relevant facts, details, and/or explanations
-includes a variety of sentence types
-contains some errors in the conventions of the English language (grammar, punctuation, capitalization, spelling). These errors do not interfere with the reader's understanding of the writing.

2 **Emerging**
-addresses only parts of the writing tasks
-demonstrates little understanding of purpose
-maintains an inconsistent point of view, focus, and/or organizational structure
-suggests a central idea with limited facts, details, and/or explanations
-includes little variety in sentence types
-contains several errors in the conventions of the English language (grammar, punctuation, capitalization, spelling). These errors may interfere with the reader's understanding of the writing.

1 **No Evidence**
-addresses only one part of the writing task
-demonstrates no understanding of purpose
-lacks a clear point of view, focus, and/or organizational structure
-lacks a central idea but may contain marginally related facts, details, and/or explanations
-includes no sentence variety
-contains serious errors in the conventions of the English language (grammar, punctuation, capitalization, spelling). These errors interfere with the reader's understanding of the writing.

4th Grade Writing Rubric

Exemplary
-clearly addresses all parts of the writing task
-demonstrates a clear understanding of purpose
-maintains a consistent point of view, focus, and organizational structure, including paragraphing when appropriate
-includes a clearly presented central idea with relevant facts, details, and/or explanations
-includes a variety of sentence types
-contains few, if any, errors in the conventions of the English language (grammar, punctuation, capitalization, spelling). These errors do not interfere with the reader's understanding of the writing.

Mastery
-addresses all parts of the writing task
-demonstrates a general understanding of purpose
-maintains a mostly consistent point of view, focus, and organizational structure, including paragraphing when appropriate
-presents a central idea with mostly relevant facts, details, and/or explanations
-includes a variety of sentence types
-contains some errors in the conventions of the English language (grammar, punctuation, capitalization, spelling). These errors do not interfere with the reader's understanding of the writing.

Emerging
-addresses only parts of the writing tasks
-demonstrates little understanding of purpose
-maintains an inconsistent point of view, focus, and/or organizational structure
-suggests a central idea with limited facts, details, and/or explanations
-includes little variety in sentence types
-contains several errors in the conventions of the English language (grammar, punctuation, capitalization, spelling). These errors may interfere with the reader's understanding of the writing.

No Evidence
-addresses only one part of the writing task
-demonstrates no understanding of purpose
-lacks a clear point of view, focus, and/or organizational structure
-lacks a central idea but may contain marginally related facts, details, and/or explanations
-includes no sentence variety
-contains serious errors in the conventions of the English language (grammar, punctuation, capitalization, spelling). These errors interfere with the reader's understanding of the writing.

4th Grade Writing Rubric

4 **Exemplary**
-clearly addresses all parts of the writing task
-demonstrates a clear understanding of purpose
-maintains a consistent point of view, focus, and organizational structure, including paragraphing when appropriate
-includes a clearly presented central idea with relevant facts, details, and/or explanations
-includes a variety of sentence types
-contains few, if any, errors in the conventions of the English language (grammar, punctuation, capitalization, spelling). These errors do not interfere with the reader's understanding of the writing.

3 **Mastery**
-addresses all parts of the writing task
-demonstrates a general understanding of purpose
-maintains a mostly consistent point of view, focus, and organizational structure, including paragraphing when appropriate
-presents a central idea with mostly relevant facts, details, and/or explanations
-includes a variety of sentence types
-contains some errors in the conventions of the English language (grammar, punctuation, capitalization, spelling). These errors do not interfere with the reader's understanding of the writing.

2 **Emerging**
-addresses only parts of the writing tasks
-demonstrates little understanding of purpose
-maintains an inconsistent point of view, focus, and/or organizational structure
-suggests a central idea with limited facts, details, and/or explanations
-includes little variety in sentence types
-contains several errors in the conventions of the English language (grammar, punctuation, capitalization, spelling). These errors may interfere with the reader's understanding of the writing.

1 **No Evidence**
-addresses only one part of the writing task
-demonstrates no understanding of purpose
-lacks a clear point of view, focus, and/or organizational structure
-lacks a central idea but may contain marginally related facts, details, and/or explanations
-includes no sentence variety
-contains serious errors in the conventions of the English language (grammar, punctuation, capitalization, spelling). These errors interfere with the reader's understanding of the writing.

Figure 62. Cut the four individual rubrics apart after being photocopied onto an 8 1/2 x 11 sheet of paper.

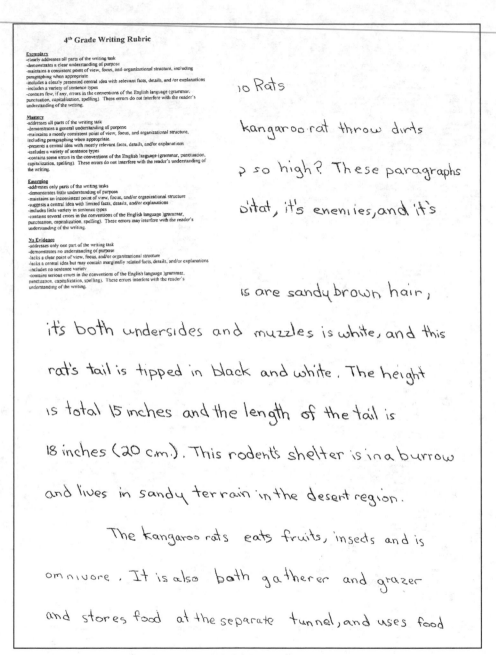

4th Grade Writing Rubric

Exemplary
-clearly addresses all parts of the writing task
-demonstrates a clear understanding of purpose
-maintains a consistent point of view, focus, and organizational structure, including paragraphing when appropriate
-includes a clearly presented central idea with relevant facts, details, and /or explanations
-includes a variety of sentence types
-contains few, if any, errors in the conventions of the English language (grammar, punctuation, capitalization, spelling). These errors do not interfere with the reader's understanding of the writing.

Mastery
-addresses all parts of the writing task
-demonstrates a general understanding of purpose
-maintains a mostly consistent point of view, focus, and organizational structure, including paragraphing when appropriate.
-presents a central idea with mostly relevant facts, details, and/or explanations
-includes a variety of sentence types
-contains some errors in the conventions of the English language (grammar, punctuation, capitalization, spelling). These errors do not interfere with the reader's understanding of the writing.

Emerging
-addresses only parts of the writing tasks
-demonstrates little understanding of purpose
-maintains an inconsistent point of view, focus, and/or organizational structure
-suggests a central idea with limited facts, details, and/or explanations
-includes little variety in sentence types
-contains several errors in the conventions of the English language)grammar, punctuation, capitalization, spelling). These errors may interfere with the reader's understanding of the writing.

No Evidence
-addresses only one part of the writing task
-demonstrates no understanding of purpose
-lacks a clear point of view, focus, and/or organizational structure
-lacks a central idea but may contain marginally related facts, details, and/or explanations
-includes no sentence variety
-contains serious errors in the conventions of the English language)grammar, punctuation, capitalization, spelling). These errors interfere with the reader's understanding of the writing.

10 Rats

kangaroo rat throw dirts

? so high? These paragraphs

bitat, it's enemies, and it's

is are sandy brown hair,

it's both undersides and muzzles is white, and this

rat's tail is tipped in black and white. The height

is total 15 inches and the length of the tail is

18 inches (20 cm.). This rodent's shelter is in a burrow

and lives in sandy terrain in the desert region.

The kangaroo rats eats fruits, insects and is

omnivore. It is also both gatherer and grazer

and stores food at the separate tunnel, and uses food

Figure 63. Staple one rubric to the assignment.

Alternatively, you could cut your rubrics in such a way as to have two of the same rubric stapled to each assignment. Have students score their work themselves or trade and score with a partner, then the teacher can score the other rubric. This creates an opportunity to have a discussion with the child and to examine what they think they need to work on versus what you think they need to work on. Again, this gives the teacher an insight into how the student heard and understood the instruction and how the student applies and generalizes knowledge. The two rubrics can be on a half sheet of paper, and stapled to the assignment. Another use for this type of scoring system is to have the parent score a take-home project and then the child can score himself as well. As the teacher, this gives you an insight into parental expectations and gives you material to discuss with the parents. It also lets the child and parent reflect on how well the project was completed and see if all directions were followed.

The following figure shows how a rubric can be printed so that one side can be scored by the student and one side can be scored by the teacher.

Student rubric for scoring (name) _____ General Writing Rubric (Grades 3-6)	Teacher rubric for scoring General Writing Rubric (Grades 3-6)
4 – Exemplary • clearly addresses all parts of the writing task • demonstrates a clear understanding of purpose • maintains a consistent point of view, focus, and organizational structure, including paragraphing when appropriate • includes a clearly presented central idea with relevant facts, details, and/or explanations • includes a variety of sentence types • contains zero errors in English language conventions (grammar, punctuation, capitalization, spelling)	4 – Exemplary • clearly addresses all parts of the writing task • demonstrates a clear understanding of purpose • maintains a consistent point of view, focus, and organizational structure, including paragraphing when appropriate • includes a clearly presented central idea with relevant facts, details, and/or explanations • includes a variety of sentence types • contains zero errors in English language conventions (grammar, punctuation, capitalization, spelling)

cont.

3 – Mastery	3 – Mastery
• addresses all parts of the writing task	• addresses all parts of the writing task
• demonstrates a general understanding of purpose	• demonstrates a general understanding of purpose
• maintains a mostly consistent point of view, focus, and organizational structure, including paragraphing when appropriate	• maintains a mostly consistent point of view, focus, and organizational structure, including paragraphing when appropriate
• presents a central idea with mostly relevant facts, details, and/or explanations	• presents a central idea with mostly relevant facts, details, and/or explanations
• includes some variety in sentence types	• includes some variety in sentence types
• contains some errors in English language conventions (grammar, punctuation, capitalization, spelling). The errors do not interfere with the reader's understanding of the writing.	• contains some errors in English language conventions (grammar, punctuation, capitalization, spelling). The errors do not interfere with the reader's understanding of the writing.
2 – Approaching	2 – Approaching
• addresses most parts of the writing task	• addresses most parts of the writing task
• demonstrates some understanding of purpose	• demonstrates some understanding of purpose
• maintains an inconsistent point of view, focus, and organizational structure, including paragraphing when appropriate	• maintains an inconsistent point of view, focus, and organizational structure, including paragraphing when appropriate
• suggests a central idea with limited facts, details, and/or explanations	• suggests a central idea with limited facts, details, and/or explanations
• includes little variety in sentence types	• includes little variety in sentence types
• contains many errors in English language conventions (grammar, punctuation, capitalization, spelling). The errors interfere with the reader's understanding of the writing.	• contains many errors in English language conventions (grammar, punctuation, capitalization, spelling). The errors interfere with the reader's understanding of the writing.

cont.

1 – Emerging	1 – Emerging
• addresses one part of the writing task	• addresses one part of the writing task
• demonstrates little understanding of purpose	• demonstrates little understanding of purpose
• lacks a clear point of view, focus, and organizational structure, including paragraphing when appropriate	• lacks a clear point of view, focus, and organizational structure, including paragraphing when appropriate
• lacks a central idea with most but may contain marginally related facts, details, and/or explanations	• lacks a central idea with most but may contain marginally related facts, details, and/or explanations
• includes no variety in sentence types	• includes no variety in sentence types
• contains serious errors in English language conventions (grammar, punctuation, capitalization, spelling). The errors interfere with the reader's understanding of the writing.	• contains serious errors in English language conventions (grammar, punctuation, capitalization, spelling). The errors interfere with the reader's understanding of the writing.
0 – No Evidence	0 – No Evidence
• no paper turned in or incomplete	• no paper turned in or incomplete
• paper cannot be read due to serious conventional errors, or does not make sense	• paper cannot be read due to serious conventional errors, or does not make sense

Figure 64.

Teacher Reflection

Rubrics are also a valid reflection tool for the educator, pointing out the educator's instructional strengths and weaknesses.

All of the objectives of a task or assessment are listed in a rubric. When the teacher scores the assessment or task, she will check off that the student achieved each objective. If most of the class missed one of the objectives stated in the rubric, the teacher will realize it may be because of ineffective instruction. Likewise, if most of the class understood the instruction and achieved the objective, the teacher knows she taught the lesson well.

Breaking Down Scores

When looking at the scores the class has received on an assignment, statistically, the scores should fall along a bell curve. Bell curves of statistics mandate that the majority of students will fall into the 2 or 3 range of the rubric, with a few students going above and beyond for a 4, and a few students scoring a 1. If the majority of your students fall into the 4 or 1 range, you will need to reassess your teaching and examine how the material was taught or how the assessment was designed.

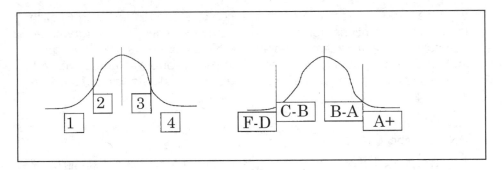

Figure 65. A bell curve applies to rubric scores in the same manner it does to traditional letter grades.

Of course, we want to see our students all receive 3's and 4's. If they have earned 3's and 4's according to the rubric, then give the score to them. Again, be clear and uniform with the format and use of your rubrics, to ensure consistency.

Discussion Questions

1. How do you encourage a "safe" sense of community within your classroom? Are your students familiar with the process of consensus building? How can you integrate the process of building consensus into other curricular areas?
2. In your experience, is it realistic for middle and high schools to use rubrics? Support your claim.

3. Design an assessment and rubric (any subject area) that includes more than one standard. Use a specific example, including standards from your teaching. Discuss how your students could help you design this rubric.

Inform

School Change

When designing rubrics be aware of your site assessment plan (scope and sequence). There should be continuity within the grade level as well as between grade levels to ensure valid data. Teachers should establish universal wording for score levels and teachers should have a shared understanding of the level of achievement required for each score level.

When implementing a new system at any school, administrators must support the program by providing teacher release time reserved specifically for training teachers and giving them the opportunity to discuss the new concepts and to share their experiences with the implementation process, student work, and instructional practices.

Because the process of changing over your grading system is an in-depth process that can take a long time to establish, a school may want to phase in just one curricular area to use with rubrics. Once the staff is comfortable using them, start phasing in the other subject areas.

Informing Instruction

Keeping accurate records of student achievement and assessment scores is vital. The point of assessing students is to inform instruction, and to ultimately ensure students' mastery of academic content areas. Teachers have a personal responsibility to be familiar with their students' strengths and areas of need, and to have the ability to communicate that academic knowledge to others. Teachers must be able to discuss each student as an individual with each child's parents or guardians, and the administration. Teachers must be able to design and implement curriculum that meets each child's developmental level and yet ensures that each child is able to demonstrate mastery of the required academic standards. Our experience has been that rubric scoring of assessments enables us to look at each child as an individual and yet measure overall mastery of the academic standard being taught and assessed.

Mastery of a concept implies the ability to evaluate, synthesize, and apply knowledge to a task at grade level expectation. The rubric will allow you, as the teacher, to know what standards or portion of a specific standard the students have mastered. Then use that information to inform instruction. If students show deficits in certain standards, it is a concern that can be addressed with re-teaching. If students excel in other standards, you can provide them with opportunities to extend their knowledge.

Grade Books

Traditional grades, whether A through F, Satisfactory/Not Satisfactory, or percentage correct, all demonstrate what students remember from previous lessons or readings and what that student can replicate on a test. We all remember the sinking feeling in our stomachs as we looked at a failing percentage on a math test or a low grade on an essay, and the feeling of not understanding what we should have done to get a higher grade.

For easy record keeping, we have designed a special addition for grade books to record scores when using standards and rubrics. We set up grade books with each standard in the assignment column instead of the names of different activities. Created in a simple spreadsheet program on a computer, the vertical column lists the identifying number of the standard next to a short description of the standard. The horizontal column at the top is numbered for each student. You could leave the number to identify each student, or you can add in the names. This allows us to know what standards have been taught and assessed.

California State Standards	1	2	3	4	5	6	7	8	9	10	11	12
1.0 Number Sense												
1.1 Read and write whole numbers												
1.2 Order and compare												
1.3 Rounding												
1.4 Decide when to round and explain												
1.5 Interpretations of fractions												
1.6 Write tenths and hundredths												
1.7 Representation of fractions												
1.8 Negative numbers												
1.9 Number line												
2.0 Decimals												
2.1 Estimate and compute to 2 places												
2.2 Round 2 place decimals												
3.0 Problem solving												
3.1 adding and subtracting multidigits												
3.2 Algorithms mult. And div.(1 digit)												
3.3 Mult. By 2 digit numbers												
3.4 Division by 1 digit numbers												
4.0 Factoring small numbers												
4.1 Break down whole numbers												
4.2 Prime numbers												
Algebra and Functions												
1.0 Use and interpret variables												
1.1 Use symbols												
1.2 Interpret and evaluate parentheses												
1.3 Use parentheses												
1.4 Use formulas												
1.5 Use equations												
2.0 Manipulate equations												
2.1 Equals added to equals are equal												
2.2 Equals mult. By equals are equal												
Measurement and Geometry												
1.0 Perimeter and area												
1.1 Area of rectangles												
1.2 Same area, diff. Perimeter												
1.3 Same perimeter, diff. Area												
1.4 use formulas												

cont

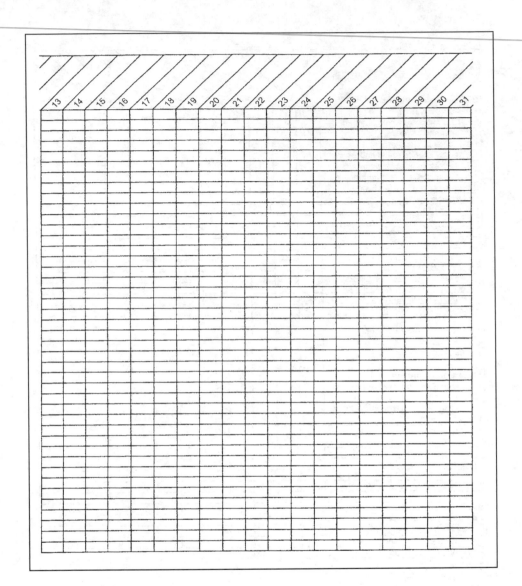

Figure 66. An example of a 4th grade teacher grade book.

The idea of using rubrics with standards is that the activities leading up to the assessment are for practice, whereas the final score the child receives is for the final assessment given for the particular standard. This is not to say practice activities are not worthy of a recorded score but we assume kids need practice and may not perform to the best of their ability when first being introduced to a concept. For record keeping of these activities like practice worksheets, whole class activities, and homework, create a separate section in the grade book, as these activities still contribute to grades reserved for participation and completing class assignments. They can also be kept as a practical application of ongoing work portfolios.

Once students have had ample practice with a particular skill or application of a standard, the standard can be assessed. This assessment is a valid measure of the child's application of the knowledge gained; this is the only score that needs to be entered into the grade book. A grade book that counts all tasks (practice and assessments) is an average of a child's performance from when the skill was first introduced through the assessment. We want the final score given to a child to reflect their knowledge at the end of the teaching period; that is, what that student has learned and can apply.

Here is an example for a student who was learning about rounding numbers. These scores were given for practice activities for one student: 2, 2, 3, 2, 3. The student scored a 3 on the assessment. Although the assessment is weighted, when the other activities are averaged in to give a final score for rounding numbers, the score will be lower because of the 2's the child scored on the practice activities. The 3 on the final assessment conveys that the child has mastered the material. Therefore, it would imply the material that scored a 2 has now been learned by the child. The child should be given a 3 since he has demonstrated mastery of that material.

With rubrics we are interested in the final product. What has the child ultimately learned? If the child has received a low score on practice activities, but has since learned the material and demonstrated mastery on the assessment, then we are confident the child knows the material and should receive a score that reflects his performance. Of course this is valid if the items on the assessment resemble the items on the practice activities. The assessment should test what the child has been practicing.

A final assessment doesn't necessarily have to be in the form of a formal test. Many times we give performance tasks as assessments because it allows children to apply the knowledge they learned. A project or long-term assignment is given as the final assessment or as part of the final grade. If you give a long-term assignment as well as a test, you could average scores for the final grade. If the project results from a differentiated project, it should be noted and scored appropriately as well (see more about differentiated projects in the section regarding Exemplary work). Be thoughtful when grading projects completed at home. This may not reflect a child's ability to master the standard, but rather the parents' ability to master the standard.

Portfolios

We must also be able to demonstrate a child's growth and change over time, so in addition to creating and using rubrics, we advocate the implementation of student work portfolios and keeping work samples over the course of several years. A portfolio is a collection of a student's work that shows growth in a subject area and shows some of the student's favorite assignments. A portfolio also provides students, parents, and teachers with another form of ongoing evaluation and an interactive communication tool. So many times a student will bring home a poor score on a science test and it may look as though the child is not doing well in the subject. Being able to view a portfolio with the science test as well as other activities like labs or experiments may show that although the child had a hard time with the test, the other activities show growth and understanding. Another option for portfolio work is to put both the pre-test and post-test in the portfolio. The pre-test usually shows the child has little knowledge of the standard because it has not yet been taught. After the material has been taught and the student has been assessed, it is apparent how much growth they have made. For students to visually see the change between the two tests lets them see that learning took place.

Schools may have guidelines in place already for what goes into the portfolio. We suggest students should be given some choice as to what goes in their portfolio. Maybe there were two big projects in language arts. Instead of including both, the child can look over both completed assignments and rubrics and see which one they are more proud of or which one had a bigger impact on them.

Evaluation of students' work and progress can take many forms. We suggest having multiple forms of evaluation like rubrics, portfolios, report cards, and standardized testing.

What if I Use Rubrics but Have to Give Letter Grades?

Rubrics show what parts of the goal the child has mastered and which things the child is still working towards. A 3 on a rubric does not translate to a B or a C.

The comment some teachers make is that giving a B on a report card for the one overall subject of math is actually about the same as giving a 2 for number sense, a 3 for algebra, and a 2 for problem solving. Remember, rubrics do not just provide an evaluation of a student's performance, but should provide specific information about a student's achievement on a specific standard or task. If we, as teachers do not provide specific information about what our students are excelling in and what they need to work on, our students will never achieve the academic growth we hope for.

Within a school, district, or state, a 4 should look the same no matter which teacher is awarding the score. Although this seems impossible to achieve, it would be beneficial and provide consistency for all children. Since descriptors are rarely given with letter grades, an A could look the same as a 1, 2, 3, or a 4 depending on the teacher, school, district, or state. Certainly if A, B, C, and D were used instead of 4, 3, 2, 1 but if descriptive components (not percent correct) were used with each letter grade, it could be done.

What Does a Completed Rubric Tell Us?

You will find students usually do not score all components in the same score levels. So what happens when some components score in the 3 and some components score in the 2? What overall score do you award for the task?

Oral Presentations – Grade 5
Narrative
Speaking Applications Standard 2.1
Listening and Speaking Strategies Standards 1.4, 1.5, 1.6

4 – Exemplary
- Student selects an appropriate focus, organizational structure, and point of view for an oral presentation.
- Student consistently clarifies and supports spoken ideas with evidence and examples.
- Student consistently engages the audience with appropriate verbal cues, facial expressions, and gestures.
- Student establishes a situation, plot, point of view, and setting with descriptive words and phrases.
- Student consistently shows, rather than tells, the listener what happens.

---

cont.

3 – Mastery
- Student selects a focus, organizational structure, and point of view for an oral presentation.
- Student clarifies and supports spoken ideas with evidence and examples most of the time.
- Student engages the audience with appropriate verbal cues, facial expressions, and gestures most of the time.
- Student establishes a situation, plot, point of view, and setting.
- Student shows, rather than tells, the listener what happens most of the time.

2 – Approaching
- Student may not select one of the following: a focus, organizational structure, and point of view for an oral presentation.
- Student clarifies and supports spoken ideas with evidence and examples some of the time.
- Student engages the audience with appropriate verbal cues, facial expressions, and gestures some of the time.
- Student may not establish one of the following: situation, plot, point of view, or setting.
- Student shows, rather than tells, the listener what happens some of the time.

1 – Emerging
- Student may not select more than one or more of the following: a focus, organizational structure, and point of view for an oral presentation.
- Student does not clarify or support spoken ideas with evidence and examples.
- Student does not engage the audience with appropriate verbal cues, facial expressions, and gestures.
- Student does not establish one or all of the following: situation, plot, point of view, or setting.
- Student shows, rather than tells, the listener what happens most of the time.

0 – No Evidence
- Student does not have a presentation prepared or presentation is incomplete.

Figure 67. Most components are highlighted in the score level 3.

Although the rubric from Figure 67 has one component highlighted in the 4 score level, the majority of the components are highlighted in the 3 score level. What score would you award this student? Is it more of a 3 or more of a 4? Because the majority of achievement is within the mastery category that is the score he will receive. This implies all components are of equal weight or value. If you find some components or standards are more heavily weighted, or there is too much information in one standard, try to separate them out into multiple components to ensure all are of equal value. This is quite important to ensure the rubrics are a valid measure of the students' ability. One component in the mastery score level could be "Has a logical title" and another component could be "Student maintains a mostly consistent point of view, focus, and organizational structure, including paragraphing when appropriate." Clearly these two components, although relevant to assessment, are weighted differently. Coming up with a title is a lot less work and effort than writing with a consistent point of view and organizational structure. If your components seem to differ in weight, break them up into multiple components.

Some teachers give pluses and minuses with rubric scores. This is acceptable if your school has decided to use pluses and minuses. The question then arises "how do you decide if a plus or minus needs to be awarded with the score?" This adds subjectivity, so be consistent and thoughtful if your school does this. Using the above example, one could argue all components were mastery quality or better. This could render a score of 3+. We suggest if you use pluses and minuses that there has to be at least two components highlighted in the category that would award the plus or minus. The rubric in Figure 67 would then score a 3. Using the same rubric from Figure 67, we would suggest the scores in Figure 68 if you are using pluses and minuses.

In Figure 68, since the majority of highlighted components are in the 3, the base score would be a 3. There are two components highlighted in the 4 so we will add a plus to the score to give a final score of 3+.

Oral Presentations – Grade 5
Narrative
Speaking Applications Standard 2.1
Listening and Speaking Strategies Standards 1.4, 1.5, 1.6

4 – Exemplary
- Student selects an appropriate focus, organizational structure, and point of view for an oral presentation.
- Student consistently clarifies and supports spoken ideas with evidence and examples.
- Student consistently engages the audience with appropriate verbal cues, facial expressions, and gestures.
- Student establishes a situation, plot, point of view, and setting with descriptive words and phrases.
- Student consistently shows, rather than tells, the listener what happens.

3 – Mastery
- Student selects a focus, organizational structure, and point of view for an oral presentation.
- Student clarifies and supports spoken ideas with evidence and examples most of the time.
- Student engages the audience with appropriate verbal cues, facial expressions, and gestures most of the time.
- Student establishes a situation, plot, point of view, and setting.
- Student shows, rather than tells, the listener what happens most of the time.

2 – Approaching
- Student may not select one of the following: a focus, organizational structure, and point of view for an oral presentation.
- Student clarifies and supports spoken ideas with evidence and examples some of the time.
- Student engages the audience with appropriate verbal cues, facial expressions, and gestures some of the time.
- Student may not establish one of the following: situation, plot, point of view, or setting.
- Student shows, rather than tells, the listener what happens some of the time.

cont.

1 – Emerging
- Student may not select more than one or more of the following: a focus, organizational structure, and point of view for an oral presentation.
- Student does not clarify or support spoken ideas with evidence and examples.
- Student does not engage the audience with appropriate verbal cues, facial expressions, and gestures.
- Student does not establish one or all of the following: situation, plot, point of view, or setting.
- Student shows, rather than tells, the listener what happens most of the time.

0 – No Evidence
- Student does not have a presentation prepared or presentation is incomplete.

Figure 68. Most components are highlighted in the score level 3 but still have two components highlighted in the score level 4.

Oral Presentations – Grade 5
Narrative
Speaking Applications Standard 2.1
Listening and Speaking Strategies Standards 1.4, 1.5, 1.6

4 – Exemplary
- Student selects an appropriate focus, organizational structure, and point of view for an oral presentation.
- Student consistently clarifies and supports spoken ideas with evidence and examples.
- Student consistently engages the audience with appropriate verbal cues, facial expressions, and gestures.
- Student establishes a situation, plot, point of view, and setting with descriptive words and phrases.
- Student consistently shows, rather than tells, the listener what happens.

3 – Mastery
- Student selects a focus, organizational structure, and point of view for an oral presentation.

cont.

- Student clarifies and supports spoken ideas with evidence and examples most of the time.
- Student engages the audience with appropriate verbal cues, facial expressions, and gestures most of the time.
- Student establishes a situation, plot, point of view, and setting.
- Student shows, rather than tells, the listener what happens most of the time.

2 – Approaching
- Student may not select one of the following: a focus, organizational structure, and point of view for an oral presentation.
- Student clarifies and supports spoken ideas with evidence and examples some of the time.
- Student engages the audience with appropriate verbal cues, facial expressions, and gestures some of the time.
- Student may not establish one of the following: situation, plot, point of view, or setting.
- Student shows, rather than tells, the listener what happens some of the time.

1 – Emerging
- Student may not select more than one or more of the following: a focus, organizational structure, and point of view for an oral presentation.
- Student does not clarify or support spoken ideas with evidence and examples.
- Student does not engage the audience with appropriate verbal cues, facial expressions, and gestures.
- Student does not establish one or all of the following: situation, plot, point of view, or setting.
- Student shows, rather than tells, the listener what happens most of the time.

0 – No Evidence
- Student does not have a presentation prepared or presentation is incomplete.

Figure 69. Most components are highlighted in the score level 3 but still have two components highlighted in the score level 2.

In Figure 69, since more components are highlighted in the 3 the base score would be a 3. There are two components highlighted in the 2 so we will add a minus to the score to give a final score of 3.

Oral Presentations – Grade 5
Narrative
Speaking Applications Standard 2.1
Listening and Speaking Strategies Standards 1.4, 1.5, 1.6

4 – Exemplary
- Student selects an appropriate focus, organizational structure, and point of view for an oral presentation.
- Student consistently clarifies and supports spoken ideas with evidence and examples.
- Student consistently engages the audience with appropriate verbal cues, facial expressions, and gestures.
- Student establishes a situation, plot, point of view, and setting with descriptive words and phrases.
- Student consistently shows, rather than tells, the listener what happens.

3 – Mastery
- Student selects a focus, organizational structure, and point of view for an oral presentation.
- Student clarifies and supports spoken ideas with evidence and examples most of the time.
- Student engages the audience with appropriate verbal cues, facial expressions, and gestures most of the time.
- Student establishes a situation, plot, point of view, and setting.
- Student shows, rather than tells, the listener what happens most of the time.

2 – Approaching
- Student may not select one of the following: a focus, organizational structure, and point of view for an oral presentation.
- Student clarifies and supports spoken ideas with evidence and examples some of the time.
- Student engages the audience with appropriate verbal cues, facial expressions, and gestures some of the time.

---

cont.

- Student may not establish one of the following: situation, plot, point of view, or setting.
- Student shows, rather than tells, the listener what happens some of the time.

1 – Emerging
- Student may not select more than one or more of the following: a focus, organizational structure, and point of view for an oral presentation.
- Student does not clarify or support spoken ideas with evidence and examples.
- Student does not engage the audience with appropriate verbal cues, facial expressions, and gestures.
- Student does not establish one or all of the following: situation, plot, point of view, or setting.
- Student shows, rather than tells, the listener what happens most of the time.

0 – No Evidence
- Student does not have a presentation prepared or presentation is incomplete.

Figure 70. Most components are highlighted in the score level 3 but one component is highlighted in the score level 4 and one in 2.

In Figure 70, most components are highlighted in the 3 the base score would be a 3. There is one component highlighted in the 4 and one component highlighted in the 2 so we will consider those two components to cancel each other out and award a score of 3.

Reviewing Scores/Areas of Need

Since the basis for using rubrics is to inform instruction and communication, an effective educator should take the time to review the scored rubrics after giving an assessment. This enables the teacher to identify skills or concepts that groups of students may need further instruction in. It should enable a teacher to see patterns over time, in their own teaching practice and in individual students over time.

We used our rubric scores to create "flex groups" and to help set the focus for mini lessons. Flex groups are small groups of children grouped together for instruction based on a common area of need. These groups constantly change to address children's changing needs.

The example in Figure 71 comes from a second grader at the beginning of the school year. Simply looking at the student's writing shows a lack of consistent use of conventions and a need for spelling instruction. However, the second-grade writing rubric also specifies a need for a sequence to the story, descriptive words, and a clear topic. As a result of the lack of conventions and the confusing sequence of events, this student scored a 1 on his initial writing assessment.

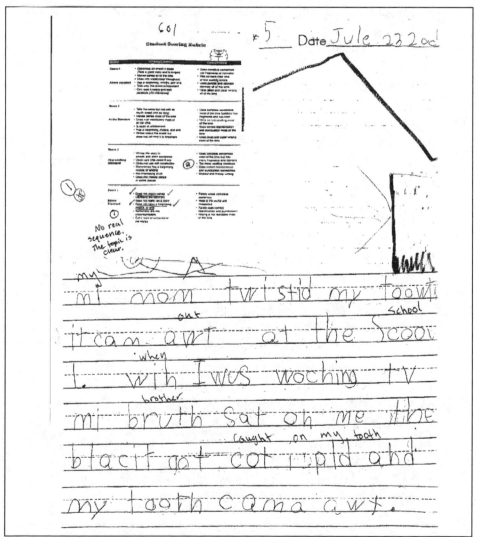

Figure 71. Second grade writing sample in August .

2nd grade Holistic Writing Rubric

4 – Exemplary (Above Standard)
- Provides a context within which an event takes place
- Provides insight into why this event is memorable/important
- Uses descriptive language (metaphors, similes and imagery)
- Has no spelling errors, including common homophones
- Consistently uses a variety of complex sentences

3 – Mastery (At Standard)
- Writes a brief narrative (WA 2.1)
- Moves through a logical sequence of events (WA 2.1a)
- Describes setting, characters, and events in detail (WA 2.1b)
- Uses descriptive language (adjectives and action verbs) (WS 1.4)
- Uses complete sentences and correct word order (WOL 1.1, 1.2, 1.3)
- Maintains consistent focus (WS 1.1)
- Uses legible handwriting (WS 1.2)
- Spells high frequency and 2nd grade sight words appropriately (WOL 1.7, 1.8)
- Capitalizes proper nouns, beginning of sentences, titles, and initials (WOL 1.6)
- Uses correct punctuation (commas in a series and dates, quotation marks, periods, question marks, and exclamation points) (WOL 1.4, 1.6)

2 – Developing (Approaching Mastery)
- Attempts to write a brief narrative
- Uses simple brief sentences
- Does not use descriptive language
- Has the beginnings of a logical sequence
- Most sentences are complete and use correct word order
- Handwriting is not consistently legible
- May have occasional spelling errors in high frequency and 2nd grade sight words
- May have occasional errors with capitalization
- May have occasional errors with punctuation

cont.

1 – Below Standard
  • Does not address the prompt
  • Mentions the event but little else
  • Lacks logical sequence
  • Lacks detail and descriptive words
  • Handwriting is illegible
  • Many spelling errors which distract the reader
  • May capitalization errors which distract the reader

Figure 72. Rubric used to score the second grade writing sample in Figure 71.

Figure 72 shows the writing rubric that this second grade team developed using the California state academic standards to score the above piece of writing. Note that the standards are marked only under the "mastery" criteria—reinforcing the grade level expectation. The second grade team also chose to score students "holistically" on their writing, rather than by identifying specific writing traits to score students on. This decision was based on the implementation of Writer's Workshop and their ongoing effort to improve the quality of student writing.

By December, the second grade team of teachers had discussed what they perceived as a "lack of progress" with this student's writing. As part of their school focus on looking at student work, they decided that the assignment and their expectations were not clarified for the students. As a result, the cover sheet in Figure 73 is what evolved.

The students had had several weeks experience re-writing the rubric into kid-friendly language, and had experienced several lessons and practice sessions that were geared directly toward the rubric/second grade expectations. As a result, the student wrote the text in Figure 74.

Name_____Tehy_____#____5____

Date_____

February Writing Prompt

Write about one perfect pet that you have or want.
It must be a real animal.

Include:

- **A topic sentence**
- **At least 3 details.**
  - ○ *Tell what your pet looks like.*
  - ○ *Tell what your pet likes to do.*
  - ○ *Tell where you would keep your pet.*
- **An ending**
  - ○ *Tell why it is your favorite pet.*

Brainstorm first below

hrmit crab

lokes like

likes to play wi-

play fi

Figure 73. Cover sheet used to explain the assignment and brainstorm ideas.

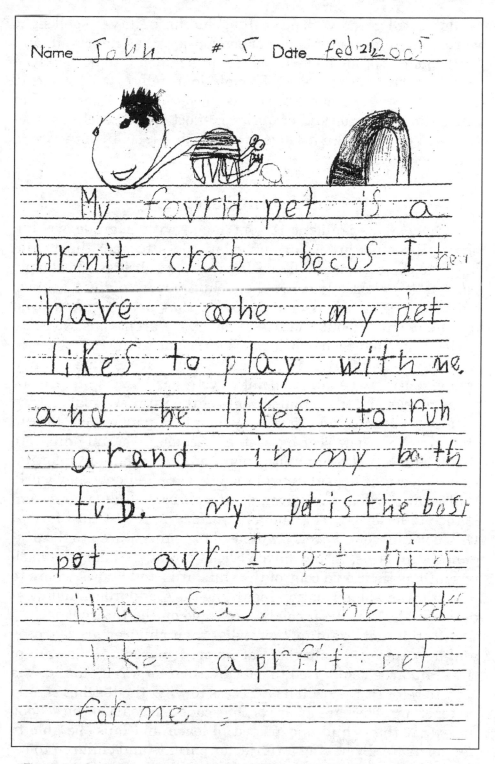

Figure 74. Second grade sample (from the same student above in Figure 71) in February.

John still needs work on spelling, but his ability to spell sight words has improved, his use of conventions has improved, and the sequence of his ideas flows. John included a topic sentence and a concluding sentence. Though John may not be meeting the second grade standard, he has moved much closer to it because the teacher used the rubric to reflect on her teaching practice, and used that knowledge to change her teaching practice to benefit the students.

Informing Parents

When an assignment is sent home with a grade written across the top, parents are often at a loss to help their child improve their grades. When a highlighted rubric is sent home, parents know exactly what their child needs to do to achieve better scores. Keep in mind, though, that parents often need to be educated about the use of rubrics. Parents also need to understand that each rubric may be specific to the task at hand and may look different from the previous rubric. This is when it is essential to be able to point to your academic standards or benchmarks and to remind parents of the ultimate goal.

Many parents and community members may be resistant to changing to a new scoring system because it is unfamiliar to them. The school community should invite parents to informational meetings to explain what rubrics are and how they work, that grades will now be given as numbers (that have no resemblance to letter grades), and as a result the report card format will look different. Parents will need to be introduced to the academic standards, if they haven't been already. Make sure each parent has their own copy of the standards and knows where to find additional information regarding the standards and/or academic goals, or make it easily accessible on the Internet.

Most parents want to know what their children are learning and how they can help them at home. If parents are aware of the standards being used to educate their children, and have a copy to refer to, they will have access to what the teacher should be teaching. They are aware of the academic goals of the school, and what their child is expected to learn and must be able to demonstrate. By having a rubric for parents and children to refer to before completing homework and other assignments, this narrows the focus to the academic standard at hand, so parents can understand what their child is expected to do and how the child will be evaluated. There are many times teachers are approached by parents who are surprised at a grade their child has received on an assessment because the student didn't study the right information or misunderstood a lesson and subsequently received a poor grade. A rubric clears any confusion as to what the requirements for mastery are.

The method of instructional planning can be shared with parents as well. Let parents know you will initiate instructional planning by examining the standards, planning the assessment, designing the rubric, then the unit of study (Wiggins, 2000). This may help the parents to understand the development process better. Let them know students are informed about the process as well and will sometimes help to generate rubrics. Use parent-teacher conferences as opportunities to re-educate parents about the informative nature of rubrics and how they can use them to help their children succeed.

In the example above, the teacher was able to conference with John's mother and not only show what John needed to work on, but also to show her John's improvement in specific areas simply by sharing the highlighted rubrics attached to her son's writing samples. As a result, John's mother was able to go home with specific goals and strategies that would reinforce the school's goal of mastering second grade writing standards.

During student led conferences, when students share their portfolios and scores with their parents, all the students were able to show their parents the attached rubrics and explain to their parents exactly what they needed to work on to improve their scores across the curricula.

Informing Students

In John's case, as with many of the students we have taught, traditional grades of satisfactory/unsatisfactory, A, B, C, D, F, or even percentage correct, do not help students focus on the specific skill that they need help with. In many cases, before teaching at a standards-based school, students were not expected to be able to identify what they needed help with.

Most students in our experience are eager to learn, when given appropriate material in a developmentally appropriate manner. Students are familiar with their parents' displeasure at unsatisfactory grades at a very young age. To give students the power of controlling their own learning and the ability to self-identify areas she needs to work on, we use rubrics as the basis for student conferences, across the curricula.

Students can be taught from kindergarten that the scoring system is a tool for their own use. During writing conferences with John, his teacher had him re-read his writing sample. When he had difficulty re-reading his own words, the teacher was able to show him his rubric. She said, "I had difficulty reading some of your words, too. So I highlighted this part of the rubric, which says 'can't read or understand the words.'" They talked about what a good story has (another second grade standard is retelling stories in order) and John remembered that a story has a beginning, middle, and end. When his teacher asked him if his story had a beginning, middle, and end, John said, "No, I forgot."

When John and his teacher concluded their conference, she told him "This was a good talk. Now I know what I need to do to help you, and you know what you need help with."

Discussion Questions

1. What steps could you take to educate parents about rubrics? How would you let them know rubric scores do not translate into letter grades?
2. Using the following final assessment and rubric, score the following student examples. What overall scores would you award? Would you give a "+" or a "−" for each paper? Would any of the children need re-teaching? Explain your choices.

General Math Rubric

4 – Exemplary
- Student consistently demonstrates understanding of math concepts beyond expectations with no mistakes
- Student is able to use multiple ways to solve a problem
- Student uses several ways to show thinking (charts, diagrams, etc.)
- Student writes clear and insightful explanations of how the problem was solved, including his or her thinking process

3 – Mastery
- Student consistently demonstrates good understanding of math concepts making few mistakes
- Student is able to use at least one way to solve a problem
- Student is able to show thinking (charts, diagrams, etc.)
- Student writes a clear explanation of how the problem was solved, including his or her thinking process

2 – Approaching
- Student show partial understanding of math concepts and makes many mistakes
- Student is able to use only one way to solve a problem
- Student is unable to show his or her thinking
- Student writes an unclear explanation of how he or she solved the problem, or is unable to explain his or her thinking

1 - Emerging
- No evidence of understanding is displayed
- No evidence of understanding is displayed in the problem solving
- Student needs individual clarification and re-teaching of concepts

Data Analysis & Probability
Grade 5

Name _____ Date _____

Create a spinner that has the following attributes:
- Has five different outcomes (red, orange, yellow, green, blue)
- Yellow is likely to be spun half the time
- Red and orange are likely to be spun the same amount of times
- Green is likely to be spun more than red or orange, but less than yellow
- Blue is likely to be spun the least amount of times

Explain why you designed your spinner the way you did. Use terms "more likely, less likely, attributes, outcome." Be sure to explain yourself using both words and numbers. Using multiple ways to solve the problem may count towards a score of exemplary.

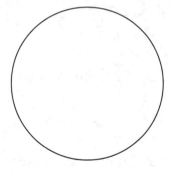

Data Analysis & Probability
Grade 5

Name Alexa Roberts
Date 3-18-04

Create a spinner that has the following attributes:
- Has five different outcomes (red, orange, yellow, green, blue)
- Yellow is likely to be spun half the time
- Red and orange are likely to be spun the same amount of times
- Green is likely to be spun more than red or orange, but less than yellow
- Blue is likely to be spun the least amount of times

Explain why you designed your spinner the way you did. Use terms "more likely, less likely, attributes, outcome." Be sure to explain yourself using both words and numbers. Using multiple ways to solve the problem may count towards a score of exemplary.

yellow is half likely so I cut the circle in half and colored it yellow. Red and orange are just as likely to be spun the same amount. I made them the same size. I made green bigger than red and orange but smaller than yellow. Green is less likely than yellow but more likely than red and orange. Blue is the least likely to be spun out of all of them so I made it the smallest piece. The probable outcome is yellow is spun the most, green the next most, red and orange next, and blue the least.

Data Analysis & Probability
Grade 5

Name Matthew R.

Date 3-18-04

Create a spinner that has the following attributes:
- Has five different outcomes (red, orange, yellow, green, blue)
- Yellow is likely to be spun half the time
- Red and orange are likely to be spun the same amount of times
- Green is likely to be spun more than red or orange, but less than yellow
- Blue is likely to be spun the least amount of times

Explain why you designed your spinner the way you did. Use terms "more likely, less likely, attributes, outcome." Be sure to explain yourself using both words and numbers. Using multiple ways to solve the problem may count towards a score of exemplary.

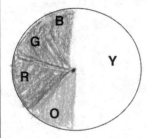

Yellow is likely to be spun half the time so I drew it half. Red and orange are likely to be spun the same so I drew them the same. Green is less than yellow but more than blue. So blue is the least likely to be spun.

For numbers if I spun 20 times

yellow — 10
green — 1
red — 3
orange — 3
blue — 3

Data Analysis & Probability
Grade 5

Name Jenny McKay
Date 9-18-04

Create a spinner that has the following attributes:
- Has five different outcomes (red, orange, yellow, green, blue)
- Yellow is likely to be spun half the time
- Red and orange are likely to be spun the same amount of times
- Green is likely to be spun more than red or orange, but less than yellow
- Blue is likely to be spun the least amount of times

Explain why you designed your spinner the way you did. Use terms "more likely, less likely, attributes, outcome." Be sure to explain yourself using both words and numbers. Using multiple ways to solve the problem may count towards a score of exemplary.

First I drew a line down the center making yellow more likely to be spun half the time. It looks like this. This is half the spinner but also 50% of the spinner because 50% is half of 100% (the whole thing). Yellow is likely to be spun 50% of the time. Then I did blue. Since blue is least likely to be spun, or spun the fewest amount of times, I just drew a small piece blue. I'm not sure what percent yet until I draw the others but it looks like this. Since red and orange are equally likely to be spun, that means they are the same size. I drew a piece about ¼ of the circle for both red and orange. Then to make them equal I just divided it in half. I got this. Since I used ¼ of the circle that's 25%. Divide it for the two colors and that's 12.5% each. That leaves the space for green already drawn. So if red and orange are ¼, then green and blue make ¼. An estimate of percents is about 6% for blue and 19% for green. This means if we spin 100 times it is likely yellow will be spun 50 times, red and orange each 12.5 (12 or 13) times, green 19 times, and blue 6 times. These are possible or likely outcomes, but it may not be what would actually happen.

3. Using the following standards and the same assignment given in question two, design a more specific rubric using the General Math Rubric as a foundation. All standards may or may not need to be included in the rubric depending on the requirements of the assessment.

Florida State Standards – Grades 3–5
Strand E: Data Analysis and Probability

Standard 1: The student understands and uses the tools of data analysis for managing information.

Benchmark MA.E.1.2.1: The student solves problems by generating, collection, organizing, displaying, and analyzing data using histograms, bar graphs, circle graphs, line graphs, pictographs, and charts.

Grade Level Expectation – Fifth
1. knows which types of graphs are appropriate for different kinds of data (for example, bar graphs, line, or circle graphs).
2. interprets and compares information from different types of graphs including graphs from content-area materials and periodicals.
3. chooses reasonable titles, labels, scales, and intervals for organizing data on graphs.
4. generates questions, collects responses, and displays data on a graph.
5. interprets and completes circle graphs using common fractions or percents.
6. analyzes and explains orally or in writing the implications of graphed data.

Conclusion

This book illustrates what a properly written rubric looks like, how to write rubrics that effectively communicate the expectations of a task, and how to use rubrics to accurately score student work. Rubrics provide both academic relevance and continuity.

This book has given you, the educator, concrete examples of both teacher- and student-created rubrics, and has shown the many different ways that implementing and manipulating rubrics can change and enhance teaching practice.

Finally, this book has shown how the use of rubrics can encourage communication between teachers, students, and parents to ensure academic success for all students. No teaching practice is absolutely "right" for any given instructor, school site, or community. We believe that any tool that encourages teachers to reflect and compels teachers to look at children as individuals, and that also promotes open communication between the school and home as rubric assessment does is invaluable and worthwhile. It is our hope that schools, districts, and states will ultimately work together to develop rubrics based on authentic student work that meets the state academic standards, and that teachers will use a thoughtful process to incorporate assessment, evaluation, scoring, planning, reflecting, and reporting.

Appendix:
General Rubrics

━━━━━━━━◈━━━━━━━━

The following general four-point rubrics can be modified to five-point rubrics to include a score level of zero. These rubrics can be used with most grade levels—kindergarten through twelfth grade—with few modifications. They are generalized in that they can be used with any assignment within the specified subject area. They have universal descriptors of applied knowledge that are used for components. This makes it easier to use with a variety of tasks, but does not necessarily specify specific standards. For example, the science rubric has a component for appropriate documentation. In any science lab or sketch, it's important to document the paper with dates for observations, or labels for identification.

These rubrics can be modified to score tasks based on your specific standards simply by changing the language and adding necessary components. These rubrics help to give you the basic components that may be required for a task. In some cases, these generalized rubrics may be fitting for your task and standards as is. But we, in no way, intend you to use these rubrics for all tasks without some modification.

General Math Rubric

4 – Exemplary
- Student consistently demonstrates understanding of math concepts beyond expectations with no mistakes
- Student is able to use more than one way to solve a problem
- Student demonstrates several ways to show thinking (charts, diagrams, etc.)
- Student writes clear and insightful explanations of how the problem was solved, including his or her thinking process

3 – Mastery
- Student consistently demonstrates good understanding of math concepts making few mistakes
- Student is able to use at least one way to solve a problem
- Student is able to demonstrate thinking (charts, diagrams, etc.)
- Student writes a clear explanation of how the problem was solved, including his or her thinking process

2 – Approaching
- Student shows partial understanding of math concepts and makes many mistakes
- Student is able to use only one way to solve a problem
- Student is unable to demonstrate his or her thinking
- Student writes an unclear explanation of how he or she solved the problem, or is unable to explain his or her thinking

1 – Emerging
- No evidence of understanding is displayed
- No evidence of understanding is displayed in the problem solving
- Student needs individual clarification and re-teaching of concepts

General Writing Rubric

4 – Exemplary
- Writing begins with a strong or creative and appropriate introduction.
- Maintains a consistent point of view, focus, and organizational structure, including paragraphing when appropriate.
- Clearly addresses all parts of the writing task.
- Clearly presents a central idea with relevant facts, details, and or explanations.
- Includes a variety of sentence types.
- Writer uses vocabulary above grade level expectation.
- Contains no errors in language conventions (grammar, punctuation, capitalization, spelling).

3 – Mastery
- Writing begins with an appropriate introduction.
- Maintains a mostly consistent point of view, focus, and organizational structure, including paragraphing when appropriate.
- Addresses all parts of the writing task.
- Presents a central idea with mostly relevant facts, details, and or explanations.
- Includes some variety of sentence types.
- Uses appropriate descriptive vocabulary.
- Contains some errors in language conventions (grammar, punctuation, capitalization, spelling). These errors do not interfere with the reader's understanding of the writing.

2 – Approaching
- Writing does not begin with an appropriate introduction.
- Maintains a mostly inconsistent point of view, focus, and organizational structure, including paragraphing when appropriate.
- Addresses some parts of the writing task.
- Lacks a central idea with few relevant facts, details, and or explanations.
- Includes little variety of sentence types.
- Vocabulary is simplistic.
- Contains many errors in language conventions (grammar, punctuation, capitalization, spelling). These errors interfere with the reader's understanding of the writing.

cont.

1 – Emerging
- No organization or focus.
- Does not address the task.
- No control of conventions.
- No attempt to explain ideas.

General Science Rubric

4 – Exemplary
- Assignment has appropriate documentation.
- Shows understanding of concept beyond grade level expectations.
- No errors in English language conventions.
- Paper is neat, organized, and easy to read.
- Assignment is complete plus additional information is added.

3 – Mastery
- Assignment has appropriate documentation, but may be missing the date or a title.
- Shows grade level understanding of concept.
- Some errors in English language conventions.
- Paper is written in a manner that is easy to follow and read.
- All components of the assignment are completed.

2 – Approaching
- Assignment may be missing appropriate documentation.
- Shows partial understanding of concept.
- Many errors in English language conventions.
- Paper may be hard to follow.
- Most components of the assignment are completed.

1 – Emerging
- Assignment has no documentation.
- Many components are incomplete or missing altogether.
- Shows no understanding of the concept.
- Serious errors in English language conventions.
- Paper is illegible.

For science labs and experiments, other components may be added depending on the nature of the task and the standards being assessed. Some possible components may be:
- All data and observations were recorded
- Student effectively used lab equipment and tools to collect data
- Student effectively displayed data
- Used data to support conclusion

General Social Studies Rubric

4 – Exemplary
- Organized into paragraphs with well-written transitions
- Includes may details to support topic and provides an in-depth analysis of the event
- All events are sequenced in chronological order
- Demonstrates above grade level understanding of the historical event
- All required information is included and possibly more information is added

3 – Mastery
- Organized into paragraphs (beginning, middle, conclusion)
- Includes sufficient details to support topic
- Most events are sequenced in chronological order
- Demonstrates grade level understanding of the historical event
- Most required information is included

2 – Approaching
- Written paragraphs, but may be disorganized or missing a conclusion
- Includes some details to support topic
- Some events are sequenced in chronological order
- Demonstrates some understanding of the historical event
- Some required information is missing

1 – Emerging
- No organization
- Includes few or no details to support topic
- Events are not sequenced in chronological order
- Demonstrates little understanding of the historical event
- Most required information is missing

For a social studies report, other components may be added depending on the nature of the report and the standards being assessed. Some possible components may be:
- Correct number of sources used
- Maps, pictures, charts, or visual aids are used
- Neatly handwritten or word processed
- Student compares the historical event with something happening in the world today
- Student explains why a historical figure may have done what he or she did and can explain his or her motivation

General Oral Presentation Rubric

4 – Exemplary
- Uses a clearly developed central idea with vivid details
- All ideas are organized and presented in proper chronological order
- A clear, enthusiastic voice is projected including, but not limited to phrasing, pitch, and modulation
- Appropriate eye contact is made at all times
- Vocabulary appropriate to the topic is used and is unique or insightful
- Uses creative and eye-catching props or visual aids (if needed or required) to enhance presentation
- Presenter responds to questions with depth and elaboration

3 – Mastery
- Uses a central idea with concrete details
- Most ideas are organized and presented in proper chronological order
- A clear voice is projected including, but not limited to phrasing, pitch, and modulation
- Proper eye contact is made
- Vocabulary appropriate to the topic is used
- Uses props or visual aids (if needed or required) to enhance presentation
- Presenter responds to questions with sufficient information

2 – Approaching
- Partial use of a central idea and concrete details
- Ideas are somewhat organized and may not be presented in proper chronological order
- A clear voice is somewhat projected including, possibly lacking phrasing, pitch, and modulation
- Proper eye contact is made some of the time
- Vocabulary not always appropriate to the topic is used
- Uses props or visual aids (if needed or required) that do not enhance presentation
- Presenter responds to questions with insufficient information

cont.

1 – Emerging
- Lacks a central idea and concrete details
- Ideas are disorganized and presented out of chronological order
- Voice lacks phrasing, pitch, and modulation; hard to hear or understand
- Little eye contact is made, if any
- Vocabulary inappropriate to the topic is used
- Uses props or visual aids (if needed or required) to enhance presentation
- Presenter does not respond to questions

General Visual Aid/Poster Board Rubric

4 – Exemplary
- Visual aid is directly related to the project
- Visual aid is attractive and creative
- All information required is present plus extra relevant information is added
- The information presented enhances provides great detail
- The information is neat and easy to read

3 – Mastery
- Visual aid is related to the project
- Visual aid is attractive
- All information required is present
- The information presented enhances the understanding of the visual aid
- The information is easy to read

2 – Approaching
- Visual aid is somewhat related to the project
- Visual aid is somewhat attractive
- Some information required may be missing
- The information presented does not completely enhance the understanding of the visual aid
- The information is somewhat neat and may be difficult to read

1 – Emerging
- Visual aid is not related to the project
- Visual aid overall is messy
- Most informational items required are missing
- The information presented does not enhance the understanding of the visual aid
- The information is illegible and hard to follow

General Book Report Rubric

4 – Exemplary
- Student can order and sequence all information appropriately
- Student can identify and provide information about the setting
- Student can discuss the main events (including but not limited to the plot, cause and effect, and conflicts)
- Student uses appropriate examples from the book to backup ideas
- Student can discuss the main characters and provide an in depth analysis of them
- Student's project is relevant to the book
- Student's project has all requirements completed correctly

3 – Mastery
- Student can order and sequence most information appropriately
- Student can identify the setting
- Student can mostly discuss the main events (including but not limited to the plot, cause and effect, and conflicts)
- Student uses examples from the book to backup ideas
- Student can discuss the main characters with details
- Student's project is mostly relevant to the book
- Student's project may have up to one requirement missing or completed incorrectly

2 – Approaching
- Student can order and sequence some information appropriately
- Student misidentifies the setting
- Student can identify some, but not all of the identified key events (including but not limited to the plot, cause and effect, and conflicts)
- Student uses some examples from the book to backup ideas
- Student can discuss the main characters, but uses little detail or explanation
- Student's project is somewhat relevant to the book

cont.

- Student's project may have more than one requirement missing or completed incorrectly

1 – Emerging
- Student can order and sequence little or no information appropriately
- Student cannot identify a setting
- Student can discuss few if any of the main events (including but not limited to the plot, cause and effect, and conflicts)
- Student uses few examples, if any, from the book to backup ideas
- Student cannot discuss the main characters
- Student's project is not relevant to the book
- Student's project has most requirements missing or completed incorrectly

Suggested Reading

Anyon, J. Social class and the hidden curriculum of work. *Journal of Education. 162* (Winter): 67–92.

Fountas, I. C., & Pinnell, G. S. (2001). *Guiding readers and writers (grades 3–6): Teaching comprehension, genre, and content literacy.* Portsmouth, NH: Heinemann.

Fountas, I. C., & Pinell, G. S. (1996). Guided reading: Good first teaching for all children. Portsmouth, NH: Heinemann

Gibbs, J. (2001, July). *Tribes: A new way of learning and being together.* Sausalito, CA: Center Source Systems, Llc.

Harvey, S., & Goudvis, A. (2000). *Strategies that work: Teaching comprehension to enhance understanding.* Portland, ME: Stenhouse.

Marzano, H., & Kendall, J. S. (1998). *Implementing standards based education.* Washington, DC: National Education Association.

Taberski, S. (2000). On solid ground: Strategies for teaching reading k–3. Portsmouth, HH: Heinemann.

Tomlinson, C. A. (1999). *The differentiated classroom: Responding to the needs of all learners.* Alexandria, VA: Association for Supervision and Curriculum Development.

Werner, L., & Bryant, P. (1989). *On the way to success in reading and writing: A second year with the early prevention of school failure program.* US Dept. of Ed. Office of Ed. Research and Improvement Ed. Resource Center

Wiggins, G., & McTighe, J. (2000). *Understanding by design.* New York: Prentice Hall.

Winebrenner, S. (2000) *Teaching gifted kids in the regular classroom: Strategies and techniques every teacher can use to meet the academic needs of the gifted and talented (revised and updated edition).* Minneapolis, MN: Free Spirit.

Winebrenner, S. (1996). *Teaching kids with learning difficulties in the regular classroom: Strategies and techniques every teacher can use to challenge and motivate struggling students.* Minneapolis, MN: Free Spirit.

Zimmerman, S., & Keene, E. O. (1997). Mosaic of thought: Teaching comprehension in a reader's workshop. Portsmouth, NH: Heinemann.

Helpful Resources and Supplemental Guides

Rubrics – A Handbook for Construction and Use (1999)
by <u>Germaine L. Taggart</u>

What is a rubric? How can I implement them as evaluation tools? How can I make better use of my existing rubrics? This bestseller answers these questions, providing all the necessary information to apply rubrics—from the classroom to the administrative office. Each chapter stands alone as a practical reference guide. The authors cover curriculum evaluation, student input into rubrics, cross-curricular approaches, rubric categories, specialty rubrics, and teacher evaluation. Easily adaptable samples, and plenty of descriptive scenarios will give educators the information and confidence they need to create, utilize, and evaluate rubrics. (www.amazon.com)

35 Rubrics & Checklists to Assess Reading and Writing (Grades K–2) (1999)
by <u>Adele Fiderer</u>

Provides a nice introduction for the use of rubrics. There are reading and writing activities with rubrics (score level 0, 1, 2, 3). The scoring "criteria" is written in paragraph form.

Rubrics for Elementary Assessment: Classroom Ready Blackline Masters for K-6 Assessment (1999)
by <u>Nancy M. Osborne</u>

125 pages of ready-to-use blackline masters, featuring rubrics for assessing performance in the elementary classroom. Includes instructions and generic format sheets for writing ru-

brics for authentic assessments in your own classroom. Gives concrete suggestions and guidelines for assessing tasks using multiple intelligences and higher order thinking skills. (www. amazon.com)

25 Fun and Fabulous Literature Response Activities and Rubrics (2002)
by <u>Christine Boardman Moen</u>
Provides literary element activities with easy to read, but vague rubrics. Geared toward grades four through eight.

Introduction To Rubrics: An Assessment Tool To Save Grading Time, Convey Effective Feedback and Promote Student Learning (2004)
by <u>Dannelle D. Stevens</u>, <u>Antonia J. Levi</u>
Geared toward higher education, including college, this book takes teachers through the process of constructing rubrics. It also gives varied forms of rubrics and a multitude of ways to use rubrics. (www.amazon.com)

Internet Resources

http://www.ccsso.org/projects/State_Education_Indicators/
Key_State_Education_Policies/3160.cfm
   Council of Chief State School Officers—Provides state content standards for all states.

http://www.lessonplansearch.com/Rubrics/
   Provides links to generate rubrics for different subject areas and activities.

http://teach-nology.com/web_tools/rubrics/
   Provides links to generate rubrics for different subject areas and activities.

http://www.ncsu.edu/midlink/ho.html
   Provides a rubric bank.

http://www.tcet.unt.edu/START/instruct/general/rubrics.htm
   Provides background information about rubrics. There is a technology section that may not be applicable to elementary classrooms.

http://www.bconnex.net/~drussell/rubrics.htm
   Assorted science and technology rubrics for comparison and revisions.

http://www.edweek.com/
   Education week on the web, and Teacher Magazine. Includes archives, daily news, special reports, and issues A-Z

http://www.m-w.com
>Merriam Webster online dictionary.

http://www.arroyovistacharter.org
>Arroyo Vista Charter School Web page, Chula Vista Elementary School District, Chula Vista, CA

http://www.cde.ca.gov/scripts/texis.exe/webinator/search?query=standards&submit=GO
>California standards and frameworks

http://www.sdcoe.k12.ca.us/score/cla.html
>Language arts cyber-guides, activities, assessment tools

http://www.rubrics.com
>Resources and templates for reference

Glossary

Academic Standards – Describe what students should know and be able to do in the core academic subjects at each grade level.

Accountability – The idea of holding schools, districts, educators, and students responsible for results.

Achievement – The quality and quantity of a student's work.

Administration – The collective body of those who manage or collectively supervise a school or school district.

Anecdotal Records – A written record, usually kept in a positive tone, of the student's progress. These could include notes, dates, and times of specific events or incidents as they occur during the school day.

Approaching – The score level on a rubric for students who have not met the standard and are performing below grade level expectation, but are showing some knowledge.

Assessment – Can be ongoing or a final test used to render a score or evaluation.

Authentic Assessment – Tasks that are worthwhile, significant and meaningful.

Backwards Mapping – Use the goal as a starting point, then developing the test that will assess that goal, finally develop the rubric that will score the test. All lessons will be planned to align with the assessment since it was designed with the end goal in mind.

Benchmarks – a point of reference from which measurements can be made.

Bloom's Taxonomy – A classification of levels of thinking created by Benjamin Bloom in 1956; a hierarchy of objectives.

Competence – Having requisite or adequate ability or qualities.

Components – The items under each score level of a rubric that are required to achieve that score.

Content Standards – Describe basic agreement about the body of education knowledge that all students should know.

Criterion-referenced tests – Tests designed to measure how thoroughly a student has learned information without comparing him to other students who have learned the same information.

Differentiated instruction – A form of instruction that seeks to challenge all students regardless of their differing ability levels. It can involve, but is not limited to, different learning environments, different assignments, and student's interest.

Emerging – The score level on a rubric for students who have not met the standard and are performing far below grade level expectation, but are showing some knowledge.

Evaluation – A single final score used to report student achievement.

Exemplary – The score level on a rubric for students who exceed the expected requirement of a task or activity.

Flex Groups – Students who are grouped together to achieve a common goal or to learn a specific standard; they are constantly changing depending on the task.

Formative Assessment – Ongoing repetitive measures designed to provide information to both the instructor and students concerning students' understanding of small segments of course material. Formative assessments emphasize mastery of course material as opposed to evaluation of performance or assignment of grades.

Grade Level Expectation – What students should know and be able to do at a particular grade level.

Independent Project – A project worked on by a student (independently) who has mastered a pretest; the project must cover the same standard as the pretest.

Interest Project – A project worked on by a student (independently) who has mastered a pretest; the project can cover any subject or standard agreed upon by the student and teacher.

Key Standards – The standards your school or state has outlined as the most important or those to be covered in depth.

Mastery – The score level on a rubric for students who complete a task or activity at the expected level. This score level means the child has met the standard.

Multiple Choice Test – Tests in which students are presented with several possible answers and are expected to select the correct answer.

Norm-referenced Tests – Standardized tests designed to measure how a student's performance compares with that of other students.

Open Ended Exemplary Section – The child comes up with a way to demonstrate her depth of knowledge to earn a score of exemplary.

Performance Assessment – A form of assessment that is designed to assess what students know by how well they perform certain tasks. Although this type of assessment is time consuming, it is worth it since these assessments give more specific information about what knowledge the child has.

Performance Standard – Level of performance sufficient for students to be described as advanced, proficient, below basic, or by some other performance level.

Performance Tasks – Activities, exercises, or problems asking children to show what knowledge they have about a certain concept. They may have to use manipulatives or draw a diagram to explain a math concept, rather than just completing a computational problem.

Prior Knowledge – Knowledge that students come to a new situation with, allowing the student to scaffold and actively construct their knowledge.

Point Spread – The number of score levels on a rubric. Most rubrics are four-point rubrics with a point spread of one through four. Some rubrics can be five-point rubrics with a point spread of zero through four.

Portfolio – A collection of student work chosen by the teacher or student to exemplify and/or document a student's learning progress over time.

Pre-Test/Pre-Assessment – A test that is given before material is taught to see what knowledge students already have on the subject matter. Can also be called a Readiness Test.

Qualifying Terms – The words used to describe each score level. The most common terms for a five-point rubric are No Evidence (0), Emerging (1), Approaching (2), Mastery (3), Exemplary (4).

Readiness Test – See Pre-Test/Pre-Assessment.

Rubric – A means of scoring and evaluating student work by which specific descriptors are listed at several different levels of quality.

Rubric based assessment – A task design based on a rubric, intended to demonstrate competency and/or areas of weakness.

Scope and Sequence – Frameworks defining curricular content and instructional strategies.

Score Level – A group of components make up a score level. One qualifying term for a score level may be "mastery" or "exemplary," whereas the score is 3 or 4.

Scoring guide – The rubric

Site Assessment Plan – The assessments that are given, recorded and weighed as part of curriculum planning and instruction at a school site.

Standardized testing – Tests that are administered and scored under uniform (standardized) conditions. Because most machine-scored, multiple-choice tests are standardized, the term is sometimes used to refer to such tests, but other tests may also be standardized.

Standards – Goals and objectives each student is expected to learn at each grade level. Each teacher is held to teaching all the standards for his or her grade level.

Standards-based education – Teachers use the standards to plan, teach, and assess lessons.

Student – A scholar or learner, especially one who attends a school.

Student Achievement – Results gained by a learner as a result of efforts.

Summative assessment – Focuses on identifying the level of student mastery and the effectiveness of instruction. Summative assessments are outcome measures that emphasize student achievement rather than aptitude or effort. From a student perspective, summative assessments are primarily utilized to determine final course grades; from an instructor perspective, they are a means of accountability.

Task-oriented assessment – Assessments that are meaningful and directly related to relevant educational material.

Teacher – The educator; one whose occupation is to instruct.

Teacher-Generated Exemplary Section – The teacher creates the question or task for the exemplary section of an assessment.

Bibliography

Bloom, B.S. (Ed.) (1956). *Taxonomy of educational objectives: The classification of educational goals: Handbook I, cognitive domain.* New York: Longmans, Green.

Cobb, C. (2003). Effective instruction begins with purposeful assessments. *The Reading Teacher, 57*(4), 386–388.

Culham, R. (2003). *6 + 1 Traits of Writing: The Complete Guide.* Portland, OR: Assessment Laboratory Network Project of the Regional Educational Laboratories.

Curriculum Development and Supplemental Materials Commission (2000). *Mathematics framework for California public schools kindergarten through grade 12.* Sacramento, CA: California Department of Education.

Department of Education. IDEA '97 General Information. Retrieved December 22, 2004. Available online at http://www.ed.gov/offices/OSERS/Policy/IDEA/overview.html

Harris, D. (Ed.) (1996). *How to use standards in the classroom.* Alexandria, VA: Association for Supervision and Curriculum Development.

Heacox, D. (2002). *Differentiating instruction in the regular classroom: How to reach and teach all learners, grades 3–12.* Minneapolis, MN: Free Spirit.

Kusimo, P., Ritter, M. Busick, K., Fergusen, C., Trunbull, E., & Solano-Flores, G. (2000). *Assessment work for everyone: How to build on student strength.* Portland, OR: Assessment Laboratory Network Project of the Regional Educational Laboratories.

O'Dell, S. (1971, March 15). *Island of the blue dolphins*. New York: Random House Children's Books.

Positive Action, Inc. How Positive Action Aligns with the Florida Academic Standards for Content Areas K–5. Retrieved May 16, 2005. Available online at http://www.positiveaction.net/content/PDFs/Florida_standards.pdf

Schools of California Online Resources for Educators. Rubrics. *Research Report*. Retrieved November 11, 2003. Available online at http://www.sdcoe.k12.ca.us/score/actbank/projectrub.html.

Theroux, P. (2002). Enhance Learning with Technology. *Differentiating instruction*. Retrieved October 2, 2002. Available online at http://members.shaw.ca/priscillatheroux/differentiating.html.

Tomlinson, C. A. (1999). *The differentiated classroom: Responding to the needs of all learners*. Alexandria, VA: Association for Supervision and Curriculum Development.

United States Department of Education. *The Facts about…State Standard*. Retrieved December 22, 2004. Available online at http://www.ed.gov/nclb/accountability/standards/standards.html

United States Department of Education. *No Child Left Behind*. Retrieved December 22, 2004. Available online at http://www.ed.gov/nclb/overview/intro/edpicks.jhtml?src=ln

WestEd. Assessments, Standards and Accountability. Retrieved on December 22, 2004. Available online at http://www.wested.org/cs/we/view/area/1

Wiggins, G., & McTighe, J. (2000). *Understanding by design*. New York: Prentice Hall.

Winebrenner, S., Espelande, P., & Rimm, S. (Eds.). (2000, November). *Teaching gifted kids in the regular classroom: Strategies and techniques every teacher can use to meet the academic needs of the gifted and talented*. Minneapolis, MN: Free Spirit.

Winebrenner, Susan, & Espelande, P. (Eds.) (1996, May). *Teaching kids with learning difficulties in the regular classroom: Strategies and techniques every teacher can use to challenge and motivate struggling students*. Minneapolis, MN: Free Spirit.

Index

Index of Figures and Rubrics

About the Authors

Jane Glickman-Bond received her undergraduate degree from Bard College with an emphasis in classical music performance, and her Master's degree in Elementary Education from Teachers College, Columbia University. She has worked with students from pre-school to adult, teaching a diverse range of learning styles and needs.

Jane currently teaches at Arroyo Vista Charter School in Chula Vista, California where she supervises the student conflict managers (Peace Patrol) and chairs the technology committee, working to integrate technology into the daily classroom curriculum.

Kelly Rose received her Bachelor degree in Liberal Studies from San Diego State, Elementary Teaching Credential from Sacramento State, and Master's degree in Curriculum & Instruction from Cleveland State University. She traveled extensively through The United States and Europe before becoming a teacher.

She taught at Arroyo Vista Charter School in Chula Vista, California where she oversaw the Safety Patrol and became a Family Science Night Trainer for the district. She currently is a stay at home mom.